SAGE was founded in 1965 by Sara Miller McCune to support the dissemination of usable knowledge by publishing innovative and high-quality research and teaching content. Today, we publish over 900 journals, including those of more than 400 learned societies, more than 800 new books per year, and a growing range of library products including archives, data, case studies, reports, and video. SAGE remains majority-owned by our founder, and after Sara's lifetime will become owned by a charitable trust that secures our continued independence.

Los Angeles | London | New Delhi | Singapore | Washington DC | Melbourne

ISRO MISFIRED

The ESPIONAGE CASE That SHOOK INDIA

K. V. THOMAS

Los Angeles | London | New Delhi
Singapore | Washington DC | Melbourne

Copyright © K. V. Thomas, 2019

All rights reserved. No part of this book may be reproduced or utilized in any form or by any means, electronic or mechanical, including photocopying, recording or by any information storage or retrieval system, without permission in writing from the publisher.

First published in 2019 by

SAGE Publications India Pvt Ltd
B1/I-1 Mohan Cooperative Industrial Area
Mathura Road, New Delhi 110 044, India
www.sagepub.in

SAGE Publications Inc
2455 Teller Road
Thousand Oaks, California 91320, USA

SAGE Publications Ltd
1 Oliver's Yard, 55 City Road
London EC1Y 1SP, United Kingdom

SAGE Publications Asia-Pacific Pte Ltd
18 Cross Street #10-10/11/12
China Square Central
Singapore 048423

Published by Vivek Mehra for SAGE Publications India Pvt Ltd. Typeset in 11.5/13 pts Adobe Garamond Pro by Fidus Design Pvt. Ltd, Chandigarh.

Library of Congress Cataloging-in-Publication Data Available

ISBN: 978-93-532-8584-5 (PB)

SAGE Team: Namarita Kathait, Sambhavi Shah, Madhurima Thapa and Rajinder Kaur

To the victims of ISRO Scandal:
Mariam Rasheeda, Fauzia Hassan,
Nambi Narayanan, Sasikumaran,
Chandrasekharan, S. K. Sharma, Raman Srivastava
and, of course, K. Karunakaran, the legendary leader,
who still live in the minds of masses.

Thank you for choosing a SAGE product!
If you have any comment, observation or feedback,
I would like to personally hear from you.

Please write to me at **contactceo@sagepub.in**

Vivek Mehra, Managing Director and CEO, SAGE India.

Bulk Sales

SAGE India offers special discounts
for purchase of books in bulk.
We also make available special imprints
and excerpts from our books on demand.

For orders and enquiries, write to us at

Marketing Department
SAGE Publications India Pvt Ltd
B1/I-1, Mohan Cooperative Industrial Area
Mathura Road, Post Bag 7
New Delhi 110044, India

E-mail us at **marketing@sagepub.in**

Subscribe to our mailing list
Write to **marketing@sagepub.in**

This book is also available as an e-book.

Contents

List of Abbreviations	ix
Preface	xi
Introduction	xiii

1. Unfolding the Story 1
2. Mariam's Tale 9
3. Fauzia, a Mother in a Telefilm 17
4. The Honey Traps and Honeybees 23
5. A Confession Video 29
6. The Bearded Man with Sparkling Eyes 37
7. The Bearded Man Weaves New Characters 49
8. The Great Scientist 61
9. Colourful Narration of a Senior Scientist 79
10. The Forced Confession 93
11. Caught by the Red Hands of Judiciary 103
12. Politics That Ignited the Fire 119
13. Game Over: CBI versus IB 135
14. The Ghost That Haunted IB 147
15. Orchestrated by and for Media 163
16. Battle of Armageddon and the Final Judgement 173
17. In Hindsight Ad Nauseam 181

About the Author	195

List of Abbreviations

AAI	Airports Authority of India
ADE	Air Defence Establishment
ADGP	additional director general of police
ASC	Arianespace Corporation
BJP	Bharatiya Janata Party
CBI	Central Bureau of Investigation
CI	counter-intelligence
CIA	Central Intelligence Agency
CISF	Central Industrial Security Force
CM	chief minister
CPI(M)	Communist Party of India (Marxist)
DE	departmental enquiry
DGP	director general of police
DIB	Director Intelligence Bureau
DIG	deputy inspector general
DPC	Departmental Promotion Committee
DSP	deputy superintendent of police
FIR	first information report
GK	Glavkosmos
GSLV	Geosynchronous Satellite Launch Vehicle
HAL	Hindustan Aeronautics Limited
HBA	House Building Advance
HEI	Hindustan Exports and Imports
IB	Intelligence Bureau

IO	investigating officer
IPC	Indian Penal Code
IPS	Indian Police Service
IR	interrogation report
ISI	Inter-Services Intelligence of Pakistan
ISRO	Indian Space Research Organisation
KPCC	Kerala Pradesh Congress Committee
L&T	Larsen & Toubro
LDF	Left Democratic Front
LPSC	Liquid Propulsion Systems Centre
MHA	Ministry of Home Affairs
MTAR	Machine Tools and Reconditions
NHRC	National Human Rights Commission
NRI	non-resident Indian
NSA	National Security Act
NSS	National Security Service
NTRO	National Technical Research Organisation
PF	provident fund
PHC	Pakistan High Commission
PIL	public interest litigation
PSLV	Polar Satellite Launch Vehicle
PUC	pre-university course
RAP	Residential Area Permit
RAW	Research and Analysis Wing
RFF	Rocket Fabrication Facility
RSA	Russian Space Agency
SAC	Space Application Centre
SC	Supreme Court
SEP	Société Européenne de Propulsion
SIT	Special Investigation Team
SLV	Satellite Launch Vehicle
SSTC	Space Science and Technology Centre
TERLS	Thumba Equatorial Rocket Launching Station
UDF	United Democratic Front
ULFA	United Liberation Front of Assam
VSSC	Vikram Sarabhai Space Centre

Preface

Whenever the TV screen flashes any breaking news or dailies come out with banner headlines on 'ISRO espionage case', the wasp inside me stirs up its wings. An aching memory haunts me as I was involved with the probe of the sensational spy case. Many times I was astounded by how facts, fiction, myth and lies are interwoven to create sensational stories or pursue vested interests of the key players of the story. Hence, after years of hibernation, I thought of deconstructing the whole episode of the espionage drama, thus this book *ISRO Misfired: The Espionage Case That Shook India*.

Through this book, I try to unravel the role of every prime character involved in the case—the 'spies', ISRO scientists, police, investigators and intelligence sleuths, politicians and media personnel—to explain how the whole spy saga was scripted for petty personal and political gains. Thus, the story is reconstructed through the interrogation statements of the 'suspects' and the first-hand information on the clandestine agenda pursued by the key players such as some politicians, investigators and media men.

As many sleuths or investigators do not desire to get identified in this sordid spy saga, fictitious names have been used in this book while narrating their role or activities. On the other hand, as the ISRO espionage story has been discussed, debated, written and rewritten for more than two decades, the names of the key players have now become a household name in Kerala and many parts of the country and abroad. Hence, such names are used as such in the book.

More than a spy thriller, I hope the readers who sincerely desire to know the inside story of the ISRO espionage case will wholeheartedly welcome and support my work.

Introduction

One more title on the infamous ISRO espionage case! Perhaps, readers might have genuine doubts that why such a book is published now, after almost two decades of the occurrence of ISRO case. So long as a spy story remains shrouded in secrecy or controversy, every now and then vested interests try to bring new skeletons out of the closet to suit their designs. On the eve of 2014 Lok Sabha polls, its echoes were heard in the political horizon when a national party coined a catchy slogan 'justice for the scientist and punishment to a top cop who investigated the case'. Similarly, coinciding with ISRO's successful Mars Orbiter Mission in November 2014, the self-proclaimed protagonists of patriotism had described the ISRO spy case as the outcome of a sinister international conspiracy to stall the progress and advancement of our space technology. Recently, Malayalam media were flooded with stories of the dubious role played by a set of senior Congress leaders in this espionage drama. Thus, day in day out, the so-called spy thriller becomes murkier. And recently, on an appeal filed by one of the victims, Nambi Narayanan, an ISRO scientist, pleading to take action against the police officers who allegedly implicated him in the case, the apex court ordered the state to pay a compensation of ₹50 lakh to him. Thus, the case once again has come to limelight and the ISRO story continues with all its mystery.

Over the years, much has been written about this spy story. Police officers, victims of ISRO case, literary/cultural figures, human/civil rights activists, progressive intellectuals, legal luminaries, media experts, politicians and religious leaders discussed and debated the case. Ironically, they stuck to their own conventional lines without making an earnest effort to unravel the mystery behind the case or bring out the truth. The print and electronic media were full of spicy stories to serve their corporate interests or to oblige their mentors. There were unending litigations—genuine and fake—by the victims as well as the police personnel and others involved in the case.

My association with the ISRO case was at different levels: initially as an interrogator, later as a liaison officer closely monitoring the litigations and related developments, and finally as a charged officer facing departmental proceedings. Despite playing diverse roles over a span of two decades, an aching memory still haunts me as to whether ISRO case was a myth or reality. Were the so-called spies imaginary characters from space? What were the real intentions of an overenthusiastic police officer who initiated the case? Whether it was to promote his career or something else? Why the premier intelligence agency endorsed his unprofessional findings and moved heaven and earth to establish an espionage case? How the Special Investigation Team (SIT) headed by a police officer described by many as an apostle of justice nakedly violated the due process of law? Was it due to his overriding ambitions to promote his professional career? What were the political and communal agendas of the key players?

But many of the aforementioned questions were settled when the Central Bureau of Investigation (CBI) exonerated all the accused without finding an iota of evidence or material on espionage or related offences under the Official Secrets Act, 1923. The Supreme Court (SC) too has acquitted all the accused, but many mysteries are yet to be unfolded. Thus, the court, while directing the state to pay compensation to Nambi Narayanan, has ordered constitution of a committee for obtaining factual scenario connected with the case.

ISRO Misfired: The Espionage Case That Shook India is an earnest attempt to look into these sensitive issues and bring out the truth by unravelling many mysteries connected with the case. Whatever included in this book are true narrations of episodes or happenings. No attempt has been made to sensationalize anything or to discredit or refurbish anybody's image. But all along an uncompromising stand has been taken to stick to the truth without any bias to any organization or individual(s). In that process, if I hurt the sentiments or image of anybody, I sincerely apologize to them. My motto is that truth ultimately should triumph.

On the other hand, I sincerely feel that revelations in this book will definitely give some solace to the victims of ISRO case, whose lives in many ways were bruised, battered and shattered for no reason of their own. The sufferings, humiliation and mental agony of these victims—their family, close relatives and friends—were quite tragic and unparalleled as manifests from the painful words of one of the victims:

'I do not want to talk about the interrogation and torture, but it keeps haunting me. My family went through a terrible time and my wife had to take treatment for mental instability. We are a loving integrated family, but the whole thing has been shattered forever. Today we are putting up a brave front, but it is just a facade, a mask which we wear even in front of each other.'

Sadly, all the dramatis personae of the scandal had paid heavily. Mariam Rasheeda and Fauzia Hassan had languished in prison for years, although no charges of espionage were framed against them. Both Nambi Narayanan and D. Sasikumaran, senior ISRO scientists, who were then working on India's ambitious cryogenic engine projects, were forced to dissociate from important assignments in ISRO. Their ordeal as accused was horrendous. No doubt, Indian space technology had its long-term adverse impact due to these developments. Two other victims, Bangalore-based businessmen, Chandrasekharan and S. K. Sharma, had virtually lost their business ventures and were in wilderness for long and recently departed from this world.

Raman Srivastava, one of the youngest Indian Police Service (IPS) officers of Kerala cadre to become IGP, was yet another victim. Just like any other senior IPS officer, he had cordial relations with the then Congress Chief Minister K. Karunakaran. But both of them had to pay heavily for these relations. Srivastava who was branded as a suspect without any basis had to face the entire ordeal within the department and outside. But he survived and later rose like a phoenix from its ashes. His links with the corridors of power in the North Block and support from sections of the IPS colleagues enabled him to tide over the greatest personal and professional crisis in his life.

But the case of Karunakaran was different. His detractors within the party and a set of leaders within the ruling coalition unceremoniously ousted him from the post of chief minister (CM) in a stage-managed image-building drama. No doubt, there were ups and downs in the political career graph of Karunakaran. However, the ghost let lose by ISRO scandal not only swallowed him but also caused unprecedented damage to the unity and cohesiveness of the Congress party in Kerala. Moreover, the scandal, one way or the other, adversely affected the political career of his son and daughter, who otherwise could prove their mettle as efficient organizers as compared with many mediocre elements of their own party holding many covetous positions. The tragedy is that ISRO scandal even haunted the progeny of the unquestioned statesman of Kerala during the last millennium!

The aching memories of this unfortunate and unethical episode still haunt the party. The wounded soul of a great patriot reincarnates as bad omen for the party and its local masters. History is repeated. Scandals, scams and schism suffocate the party. Ignominious ouster of those elevated to covetous positions after the fall of the 'leader' continues.

Who should be blamed for this? Who will own responsibility to such serious aberrations which have shaken the pillars of democratic institutions? I firmly believe that alert and democratically agile people of Kerala should seriously discuss these questions and identify the organizations, agencies and individuals responsible for such maladies.

Such an approach has now become the need of the hour. On the one hand, the threat of terrorism and extremism is posing serious challenges to national unity and integrity. On the other hand, the concept and profile of law enforcement and security agencies have undergone radical changes. The personnel in uniform are vested with draconian powers. No less is the role of those in civvies engaged in cloak and dagger operations. Blood-chilling stories of cold-blooded murders in fake encounters and clandestine operations! In fact, there is no effective mechanism to check the tendency of law enforcement and security/intelligence agencies padding up or fabricating evidence in implicating innocent persons in false cases including terrorism-related offences.

Lack of accountability and professionalism of these agencies are the main causative factors for such discreditable trends. The tragedy is that thousands of innocent citizens are incarcerated in jails as undertrials for years together. Sadly, most of them are not as fortunate as the victims of ISRO case. They are all ill-placed, resource-less, marginalized or underprivileged people. Seldom are there any organizations or individuals to raise their voice in favour of these hapless citizens. For them, concepts like public justice become a myth. Thus, the poignant question is: How can their salvation be ensured?

What will I gain out of this work? Friends or foes? Venom or vendetta of those who were responsible for the tragic plight of ISRO victims? Frankly, I am not seriously pondering over these issues. Let the readers of this book decide and find answers.

Finally, the book gives a clarion call to the civil society of Kerala that in sensational issues, it should not be carried away by the motivated propaganda. In this electronic era when the news and images instantly spread through social media such as WhatsApp and Facebook, verifying the veracity of any claims made by anyone including people in power has become very crucial. Then you can become self-ordained judges of your own. Once you are convinced, you should not be reluctant to acknowledge the reality that the victims of ISRO scandal were innocent and the hype created by a section of media, propped up by law enforcement agencies and political masters, was nothing but a myth. The civil society should once and for all renounce the machinations and manipulations being resorted to by various forces to bring ISRO case to the limelight to serve their narrow vested interests. Perhaps that would be the greatest tribute that we can give to the victims of ISRO scandal—Mariam Rasheeda, Fauzia Hassan, Nambi Narayanan, Sasikumaran, Chandrasekharan, S. K. Sharma, Raman Srivastava and, of course, K. Karunakaran. I dedicate this book to these victims.

UNFOLDING THE STORY   1

It was a pleasant evening of November 1994. The telephone rang continuously in the first floor room of my rented office cum residence at Uphill, Malappuram, Kerala, where I headed the district unit of the Intelligence Bureau (IB).

From the courtyard, I ran up the stairs and reached the first floor. The telephone was still ringing. I hurriedly took the receiver. From the other end, I heard the faint familiar voice: 'Mr Richard, you have to urgently report to the headquarters. You may be aware of the arrest of Maldivian ladies in Trivandrum. It is suspected to be a typical spy case. They have to be thoroughly interrogated'. It was the voice of the then third in command at the state headquarters of the Bureau.

I had a long association with him since he landed in Cochin office of the Bureau in 1975 after a foreign assignment. A small thin timid man full of energy and commitment. His voice choked with excitement, perhaps on the discovery of an espionage case in God's own country, which the Bureau was eagerly longing for!

'We want experienced interrogators. I have a lot of work to complete: to get in touch with outstation officers selected for the task; constitute interrogation teams and liaise with police. You know, only Kumar is with me to help. When are you going to report?'

He completed in a single breath.

'Sir, you know. I have to attend the reorientation course in Delhi for which I have made all travel arrangements. Last time, they exempted me as I was in the midst of OP-Rhino in Assam. This time there won't be any exemption. What should I do sir?'

I explained my predicament.

It was at the insistence of the Assam unit head that I got exemption from the last reorientation course. I strongly felt that it was nothing but a routine wasteful exercise regularly organized by the training institute in Delhi for the promoted officers and staff. I was not very keen to attend it, but career compulsions forced me to do so, as such training courses were linked to promotions and other assignments.

'Nothing doing, don't you know the importance of this task? You were selected by our boss. You know there would not be any excuses before him. He will talk to Delhi and settle the matter. After all it is a training programme. Nobody will chop off your head for not attending the course!'

His voice was little bit harsh.

'Ok Sir, fine. If the big boss interferes in the matter, why should I fear about the course? I will cancel the train ticket for Delhi and take a ticket for Trivandrum today itself. I will report to you tomorrow at 10 o'clock', I concluded. I sensed an element of satisfaction in the voice at the other end.'

On the ground floor where we had put up, my better half and two kids who overheard the conversation were in real shock as they sensed my absence from home for some days. They seldom had any such feelings in the past when I left them alone for weeks in remote areas amidst the threat of insurgents and militants. This time something strange had happened.

The real villain was a king cobra. His royal appearance on the ground floor hall had really terrified them. The cobra disappeared in the thin air, but they were yet to recover from the shock. An old lady from the neighbourhood rushed there on hearing the commotion. She was pretty sure that the villain had found safe asylum in the annexed room full of household goods and belongings of the house owner. On the advice of the old lady, my better half had made some quick remedies: a concoction of raw garlic and asafoetida was made and thrown inside the storeroom. The old lady was damn sure that any snake will leave its hideout due to the pungent smell of this concoction!

But that could not give them any solace. In the adjoining bedroom, with tightly closed windows and doors, we spent almost sleepless nights fearing that the king cobra will sneak in at any time. Fearful dreams of venomous cobras sneaking into the room haunted the children who woke up in the dead of night and cried in fear. My presence was the only consolation for them. Then, why should I leave them in such a predicament? That was a genuine question for which the only answer was 'duty first', the much used slogan by the senior bosses in the Bureau!

Lonely in the cabin of the night train to Trivandrum, such thoughts slowly vanished from my mind. Instead, different stories on the arrest of Maldivian ladies that appeared in the print media flashed across the mind. Some vernacular dailies hastily described them as real moles infiltrated by a hostile neighbour to collect intelligence on India's vital strategic installations including Indian Space Research Organisation (ISRO). Another story was that they were arrested for overstay in the city. Yet another version was that these ladies were on a special mission to collect information on resident Maldivians in South India plotting against Abdul Gayoom, the president of Maldives.

What surprised me more were not the contents or veracity of these stories but how the stories made headlines in the print media. Many questions came to my mind. Did the initial investigators treat the espionage suspects as petty criminals? If not, why did they celebrate their arrest sharing with the media that had sensationalized it with all spicy ingredients of a spy thriller? Whether it was due to mere publicity craze or any hidden agenda? On the other hand, if they are real spies how would the investigators adduce evidence to establish their espionage activities after such extensive leakage and exposure?

After all, even laymen have a fair idea that espionage is not like a petty theft or housebreaking offence! It is a life and death game in which the players—whether male or female—would take all precautions not to leave any telltales that would betray them. In fact, counter-espionage experts meticulously plan and launch clandestine operations for months or years to build up a foolproof case before the arrest of agents. Why such basics in unearthing an espionage network were not followed?

The train was speeding ahead breaking the thick darkness. Images of Mata Hari, Aldrich Annes, Kim Philby, etc., flashed through the mind. How meticulously they operated their espionage network? How difficult was their detection as real spies? Mata Hari, who spied for the Germans during the First World War, mingled and lived with high-ranking officers of allied forces, without a shadow of doubt. Philby, holding senior positions in MI6 of Britain, operated for around three decades before taking asylum in Soviet Union; Aldrich, a senior CIA agent, sold the most vital secrets of US and NATO powers to KGB for almost one decade before his detection. Before the science and technology made big strides, the innocent and innocuous doubts or observations by ordinary men and women who didn't know anything about the intricacies of spies and their modus operandi acted as the vital clues for counter-espionage experts who patiently and secretly pursued them leading to the sensational detection of spy networks.

Ironically, such an approach is lacking in our intelligence and security agencies which are experts at cobbling together speculations and rumours, and weaving apparently convincing espionage stories for which padding up of evidence or creation of fake documents are not uncommon. I had genuine doubts of the veracity of the widely published espionage story involving the two Maldivian ladies. My apprehensions were not unfounded when I reported at the state headquarters of the Bureau.

There was an element of excitement at the headquarters. Officers and staff were busy. On the long corridors of the office building,

lower grade staff in small groups was engaged in guarded talk. In a few office cabins, live debate was on over the media coverage of the arrested Maldivian ladies. Some young officers were quite taken in by Mariam Rasheeda, whose photograph in different postures was prominently published in almost all major vernacular dailies. Nobody took much interest in the weak, frail and pale looking Ms Fauzia.

Office vehicles were busily moving around in different directions. I wondered how the local boss who was otherwise very stringent in the use of office vehicles and petrol consumption became so lenient? He was ecstatic over the detection of an espionage case! After all, the state unit after many decades has really touched a gold mine—an espionage network having national and international linkages! Then why should he bother about petrol and vehicles?

Senior officers were weaving sweet dreams on their elevation to cosy posts, while middle level officers had their eyes on distinguished decorations and medals! The so-called computer wizards claiming themselves as super-sleuths of cyberspace were busy with the analysis of inefficacious counter-intelligence (CI) data collected by field operatives. Their main concern was to get the appreciation of the local boss who had a craze for computers and networks.

The third in command at the headquarters was designated as the nodal officer for the ISRO spy case. His room was on the first floor. Through the glass pane of the door, I noticed him inside, seriously discussing something over telephone. Kumar was also there dealing with a heap of papers. I entered the room when he completed the talk:

'Yes, then you have reached? We have to start action right now. Our teams are already on job, interrogating Mariam and Fauzia. Mr Indran, our head in Mumbai, has questioned them, already. You see, he is casual in his approach, as in the past. But Delhi people are different. They will force them to spill out the beans. After all, Bengali Dada from Delhi headquarters is supervising the entire operations. He will leave no stone unturned. Kumar will hand over the initial interrogation reports (IRs) to you. You meticulously go through them and then properly confront them.'

Before the nodal officer could complete his briefing, there was a call from the local boss. Kumar was still searching for some reports from a heap of handwritten notes.

'These Delhi people are horrible; they scribble something and throw to us and leave. Then it is our headache to properly edit it in the form of an IR and put it to the local boss.' He expressed his frustration about the haphazard style of functioning of the so-called crack team from Delhi.

'Two to three fellows from Delhi, they cannot even converse in English properly, then what to speak of their written reports in English. Then, there is our CI expert, whose written notes could not be deciphered even by a trained cipher expert.' Kumar was just ventilating his fury for entrusting him some unimportant tasks which he never did.

He searched a heap of written manuscripts and typed reports and finally located the preliminary questioning statements of Fauzia Hassan and Mariam Rasheeda. He handed over the bunch to me with a veiled warning that none should be allowed to peep into it. Typical gesture of restricted security that was taught at Bureau's training centre! Really I felt pity on him. What secrecy and security? Everything that had happened so far in the so-called ISRO espionage case had prominently figured in the columns of almost all leading newspapers published from the state!

Then it was my turn. At the corner of the room, I found a safe secluded seat. There I went through the preliminary statements of Mariam and Fauzia.

The background of their arrest as recorded was quite interesting. Suspicion against these two Maldivian ladies, as per records, had come up during the routine checking of the activities and antecedents of visiting Maldivian nationals in Trivandrum.

I felt this claim to be totally false as hundreds of Maldivian nationals visited the city and stayed for short and long periods. Some rest houses and hotels used to send the C Form containing the particulars of the visiting foreign nationals to the police, who on many instances used them as stationery for the routine writing works in the stations! But majority of Maldivians stayed in private accommodation and never furnished the details to the police. A couple of ideal residential areas in and around the city are flooded by resident Maldivians who hired houses/buildings at exorbitant rent and virtually converted them into transit camps for visiting Maldivians. There, the young and old stayed under the same roof, prepared their own cuisine and engaged in diverse vocations fully enjoying the expatriate life! While the house owners were happy, the permanent residents were distressed over the exodus of Maldivians.

Thus, the truth was something else. The special unit of police came to know about these ladies when they approached them for the extension of residential permit or other travel documents. Overstay of Maldivians has never been seriously looked into. Even the police regularized the overstay of some Maldivians for short periods on genuine grounds of illness or medical treatment. Then why was the special unit officer searching for these two particular ladies in the hotels and summoning them to the office? There was something fishy about the case, on which the vernacular media had built their fanciful stories.

But the real truth with all credentials was brought out by sections of the media: The beautiful Mariam accompanied by fragile Fauzia approached the concerned officer to extend or get regularized the former's residential permit or other travel documents. The officer apparently demanded a sexual favour from Mariam which she flatly refused for obvious reasons. This is how the whole witch-hunt started.

Then the entire drama was unfolded. Mariam Rasheeda was arrested on 20 October 1994 for overstay in Trivandrum without visa and a case vide Crime No. 224/1994 of Vanchiyoor PS was registered under Para 7 of Foreigners Order, 1948, and Section 14 of Foreigners Act, 1946. Subsequently, police registered another case against her vide Crime No. 246/94 under sections 3 and 4 of Official Secrets Act r/w section 34 IPC. Fauzia who was clandestinely taken into custody from Bangalore by a team of IB and police sleuths was shown arrested on 3 November 1994 and was detained along with Mariam.

MARIAM'S TALE

2

Away from the gossiping officers and staff, I sat alone at the corner of that spacious room and keenly went through the shabbily typed statement of Mariam and Fauzia. Going through their personal profiles, two factors prominently figured in my mind. Who will depute these semi-literate ladies to spy on the complex details of Indian space technology? Are these intelligence agencies so unprofessional? I felt the hollowness of the international conspiracy theory mooted from certain corners.

Mariam's story had all the ingredients of a Bollywood thriller. Many strange events occurred in her three decades of life. Born in South Maldives as daughter of a garment maker and an illiterate housewife, she was married to Ahmed Salim at the age of 18 while studying in Class 9. Salim was then engaged in garment and fish export.

Her marriage was short-lived. While her daughter Nishana was only 11 months old, she divorced Salim after obtaining a monthly maintenance of US$200. She was getting financial support from two of her brothers—one worked as third engineer in a Gulf shipping company and the other as a religious teacher in Malé administration.

After the death of her father, things changed drastically in her life. Her brothers insisted on her marrying Ibrahim Latheef, her cousin, who was then working in National Security Service (NSS) of Maldivian government. On her refusal, she had to quit the house of Latheef where she was staying. Then Fauzia, her distant relative, came to her help and accommodated Mariam in her house. That relation lasted for long. Fauzia also helped her to join the NSS.

In the late 1980s, she joined NSS of Malé government as a 'private'—the lowest military rank in the organization—and underwent training in the use of 303 and AK series weapons. Brigadier Ambari Abdul Sattar, the then minister of state for defence, was the chief of NSS. Iliyas Ibrahim, the brother-in-law of Abdul Gayoom, the then president of Maldives, was the deputy defence minister.

As a low rank personnel, she was mainly doing office works and was getting a monthly salary of 2,300 Maldivian Rufiyaa. Because of her ill health, especially heart ailments, she frequently availed leave and visited Colombo for medical treatment. The senior NSS officers were unhappy over her frequent leave. Thus, she tendered her resignation after serving around five years. Subsequently, her trips to Colombo became more frequent.

Mohammed Yusuf Azmi, a Sri Lankan national, came to her life in 1993 during such trips. He was engaged in garment business. Subsequently, he frequented Malé for business purpose. Later, he married Mariam and stayed in Malé for three months. As she was not willing to accompany him to Sri Lanka, he left her.

The third man who came into her life was Mohammed Arif who had some resemblance with her schoolmate and teenage lover Mohammed Samin. Arif who was married and had two children was affluent with two cargo vessels and a couple of shops in Malé. In order to overcome the legal hurdles for their marriage in Malé, they decided to visit India to register the marriage and return to Malé. Accordingly, they came to Trivandrum by air and directly proceeded to Tuticorin where one of the vessels of Arif was on visit. However, their marriage could not be registered as there was none from Mariam's side as witness to the marriage and sign the documents. Thus, after spending four days with Arif in his vessel at Tuticorin, she returned to Malé.

Incidentally, she had a weakness for any male who had any resemblance to her maiden lover Samin. After Arif, this time it was a middle-aged doctor Anand from Mangalore! During her stay in Bangalore with Fauzia, she had a chance meeting with the doctor who came to attend some ailing inmates of an orphanage run by Fr Pinto and Ms Sara Palani, the common friends of Fauzia.

She collected the address and telephone number of the doctor from Ms Sara Palani and wrote a lengthy letter to him explaining her infatuation and desire to meet him in person. The doctor was really taken aback on seeing the letter but responded through a letter which fell in the hands of the head of the orphanage. The puritan head tried to restrain the married doctor from entering into this relationship!

But lovelorn Mariam was not prepared to surrender. She continued her efforts to establish contact with Dr Anand and solicited the help of others. Fauzia who was staying with her was ready to help.

It was during June 1994 that Mariam had her second visit to India. On her trip to Trivandrum en route to Bangalore in June 1994, Chandrasekharan, the representative of Glavkosmos (GK) gate, crashed into her life by volunteering to assist her from the harassment of customs officials in the airport. They were on the same flight to Bangalore. Later in Bangalore, Chandrasekharan, by offering any help to her and Fauzia, could easily establish warm relations with Mariam. In the course of their efforts to arrange admission for Fauzia's second daughter Jila Hamdi in a better school in Bangalore, both the ladies got befriended with Sudhir Kumar Sharma, Bangalore-based contractor and friend of Chandrasekharan. In the company of Sharma, the ladies had an informal visit to an army club in Bangalore, where retired Squadron Leader K. L. Bhasin, a friend of Sharma, was also present.

Fauzia was then staying in the house of Ali Nazir, son of Ibrahim Nazir, the first Maldivian president. During that period, a large number of Maldivians were also residing in the garden city.

While in Bangalore, Mariam's meeting with her cousin sister Husang Habiba was a turning point in her life. During friendly talks, Habiba revealed a secret that her ex-husband, Abdullah Ahmed, residing at Vaniyambadi near Madras and Iliyas Ibrahim, brother-in-law of President Abdul Gayoom, based in Singapore but frequently visiting India, were planning to overthrow the president. Though Habiba passed the information to Maldivian Defence Ministry, the president was not properly apprised of this threat.

With her NSS background and contacts in that organization, Mariam tried to develop the information. Her accidental meeting with Ms Saiyeeda, the second wife of Abdullah Ahmed, at Wockhardt Hospital, Bangalore, enabled her to gather more details connected with the story. Quite cunningly, Mariam tried to create an impression that she is opposed to Abdul Gayoom regime and quit her job in NSS on this account. She also impressed Saiyeeda that Iliyas Ibrahim was the most ideal man to head the nation.

Highly impressed by her anti-Gayoom stance, Saiyeeda established good rapport with Mariam who—despite her best efforts—could not collect the former's address and telephone number. Meanwhile, Saiyeeda tried to arrange a meeting between Mariam and Abdullah Ahmed which Mariam tactfully avoided on the pretext of her urgent visit to Malé.

Mariam had successfully used the anti-Gayoom inputs that she tactfully gathered from resident Maldivians. During her visit to Malé during July 1994, she had a meeting with Abdullah Hamid, the speaker of Malé parliament and detailed about the plot by Saiyeeda and others against the president. On his suggestion, she met Brigadier Ambari Abdul Sattar, the then chief of staff of NSS, and disclosed whatever information she had about the plot. Sattar engaged her as an informer and deputed NSS official First Lt Ibrahim Latheef as her handling officer. He briefed her to furnish the details of all incoming telephone calls to her. Accordingly, she shared the details of two such calls, one from Saiyeeda and the other from Mohsin (resident Maldivian of Trivandrum working for NSS).

Meanwhile, she turned into an experienced cover agent of NSS. As per the briefing by her handler, she managed to record the conversation between her and Ali Wahid, a parliament member who was ill disposed to the president. Then, NSS tasked her to unravel the plot, especially the key players, for which she was asked to visit India. For that purpose, NSS arranged her air tickets and pocket money.

Malé–Colombo–Trivandrum route was used for her trip to India with Colombo as transit base for her operations. Thus, during the last week of July 1994, she along with Fauzia landed in Colombo. She stayed with the wife of her ex-husband's friend. Fauzia stayed with Zuhaira, wife of Daliya, a rich Maldivian having four resorts. Daliya had a second wife Ms Maizan Kadda. As Zuhaira detested Maizan, she along with her children stayed in Colombo.

However, Mohsin, who was also in the payroll of NSS, was closely monitoring her movements. On her arrival in Colombo, he also landed there and stayed in the same hotel. Though she tried to meet him in person, he evaded her under one pretext or other. Mariam with the help of diplomatic channels in Colombo kept NSS informed about his visit and her proposed trip to India during the first half of August 1994.

Just like NSS, anti-Gayoom elements were secretly monitoring her movements and contacts. Mohammed Saeed was one such element. He for the first time befriended Mariam on board the Air Sri Lanka flight from Colombo to Trivandrum during August 1994 while she was on an NSS mission. Claiming that he knew all about her and her whereabouts in Bangalore, Saeed collected her telephone number in Bangalore which was a telephone booth near her place of stay.

On her arrival in Bangalore, she visited the booth and waited for his call. She received a call from another person intimating her that Abdullah Ahmed, the leader of anti-Gayoom operations from Vaniyambadi, would meet her in person. And for that purpose, a car with driver would be sent to her place.

The conspiracy by the anti-Gayoom elements to overthrow President Gayoom, as narrated by Mariam, had all the ingredients of a well-planned coup. They arranged secret meetings with Mariam on two to three occasions in separate hideouts, briefed and debriefed her mainly to ascertain her loyalty to the 'rebels'. Mohammed Saeed played a leading role in such exercises. They enquired about her contacts with Mohsin, Ali Wahid, etc., which she could explain to their full satisfaction.

Once they were convinced of her credentials and loyalty, operational details were discussed. With the help of a sketch map, she was asked to identify and confirm strategic locations such as major police stations, NSS Office, President's House under construction, Malé Airport and an island near the airport. She was assigned a sensitive task of winning over Lt Colonel Moosa Ali Jaleel, commander of Coast Guard, to their side. When she expressed her confidence in this task, they fixed 11 November 1994 or 1 January 1995 as the target date for the operation.

In one such meeting, decision was taken to overthrow the president through a surprise attack. She was asked to go to Malé immediately to bring Jaleel to their camp. In the meantime, NSS officials maintained their contacts with her. Once at their instance she went to Vaniyambadi to meet Abdullah Ahmed, but failed to locate his house.

Her cover job for NSS was soon busted. The anti-Gayoom gang operating from Bangalore felt that she was working as a double agent and helping Maldivian Defence Ministry. Thus, they detained her at their secret hide out for three days for thorough questioning. Then she was let off with a warning that she should not dabble in their affairs. Thus, she decided to go back to Malé for which she sought the help of Fauzia to get her air tickets confirmed.

Before leaving Bangalore, both Mariam and Fauzia went to the office of Chandrasekharan to express their gratitude for all he had done to get the school admission of Fauzia's daughter. On Mariam's request to help her to establish contact with Dr Anand of Managalore, he promised to help her and referred the name of Dr Sasikumaran of Trivandrum, whose contact number was also furnished.

In Trivandrum, they stayed in Hotel Samrat. On a tip-off from Chandrasekharan, Dr Sasikumaran initially visited Mariam in the hotel along with his doctor wife who enquired about Mariam's heart ailments. But Sasikumaran, visiting her in the hotel a couple of times, established good friendship with her as a Samaritan! She narrated her old story and her deep infatuation with Dr Anand. Sasikumaran assured to help her, which strengthened their relations.

But Sasikumaran did not come in the way of Mariam's passion towards the doctor. Ultimately, he established contact with Anand and arranged a meeting between the doctor and Mariam at Calicut Railway Station during the latter part of 1994. They spent one day in the railway retiring room which was booked by Anand. After that meeting, she came back to Trivandrum and confirmed her return air ticket to Malé on 17 October 1994. In the meantime, Anand again came to Trivandrum and spent a couple of days with her. It seems after Anand left, Mariam was happy in Sasikumaran's company. On a couple of occasions, they were seen together in different hotels and resorts. With Mariam spending more and more time with him, Fauzia kept to herself.

While shuttling between Malé–Trivandrum–Bangalore, they were befriended by affluent strangers extending hospitality and entertainment. A 70-year-old Saudi businessman picked up friendship with Mariam and Fauzia at Trivandrum Airport. He took both the ladies to a star hotel where he was staying and entertained them by paying their food bills, etc. When the honeymoon with the old man was over, they shifted to a single room in Hotel Samrat, Trivandrum!

Meanwhile, in September 1994, plague struck Surat, in Gujarat, resulting in the cancellation of a number of international flights by major airliners. Mariam's confirmed return air ticket to Malé on 17 October 1994 was also cancelled. Her 90 days Residential Area Permit (RAP) had expired. Thus, along with Fauzia she went to the police commissioner's office in Trivandrum to get two days extension of stay. They submitted the extension application to the concerned officer who instead of granting the extension questioned and cross-questioned them. Both the ladies had to visit his office for three days as part of this exercise, while the overenthusiastic officer had a couple of visits to Hotel Samrat to verify their antecedents. When he heard the fancy stories about Mariam's flamboyant personal life from the hotel staff, the officer had a few dreams of his own which were soon shattered by Mariam. Frustrated over the disdain and mortification meted out by Mariam, he crafted a spy thriller with all the ingredients of money, honey trap star hotels, scientists and foreign agents! The rest was history.

FAUZIA, A MOTHER IN A TELEFILM

3

Going through the statement of Ms Fauzia was like conjuring up images of a sizzling heroine from Malé. But soon I realized how wrong my impressions about her were. Fauzia was a hapless woman who struggled to survive heavy odds in life.

Born as the daughter of a carpenter-cum-building contractor at Ussakurge, Menveru in Malé during the early 1940s, she left her studies at the age of 15 while in Class 7. Soon after, she was married to Umaru Manick. The couple had one daughter and one son. After two decades of stressful married life, she divorced her husband who was having extramarital relations with a Sri Lankan lady working as teacher in Malé. After a short stint of service in Malé Customs, she accompanied her elder brother to Sri Lanka where she picked up communication English and typing. On return to Malé, she worked as a manager of a textile shop run by NSS. Following the closure of the shop, she went to Addu Island where she found livelihood by giving tuition to school-going students and stitching clothes.

In Addu Island, she had her second marriage with Ibrahim Hamdi who was a petty pop singer. Her daughter Jila Hamdi was born in this wedlock that lasted around 10 years. After divorce, she and her daughter stayed with her father. Later, she got a plot of land from her father and constructed a house which was let out on rent. In the meantime, she played the role of a mother in a telefilm *Fida*. But she could not establish herself in the film industry.

After the death of her father, she left Malé for Sri Lanka. In Colombo, she initially stayed with Ms Yasmin as a paying guest and later hired one-room accommodation of Ms Zuhaira, a Maldivian national. Jila Hamdi was admitted in a school in Colombo. Fauzia stayed there for about three years. After admitting her daughter in a boarding school in Colombo, she returned to Malé and stayed with her sister Raziya Hassan. In the early 1990s, she used to visit Colombo in connection with the treatment of her close relatives.

Meanwhile, Fauzia along with Paya (sister of Yasmin) and her aunty visited Madras during the last week of January 1994 for shopping in connection with the marriage of Paya's daughter. After a brief stay in Colombo, she went back to Malé in the first week of February 1994. Then she was shuttling between Malé and Colombo for more than three months for the treatment of her relatives/friends.

Fauzia's son Nasif who had been to Bangalore in late 1993 suggested to her that Jila Hamdi should be put in a better school in Bangalore. He had high opinion about Bishop Cotton School there. Thus, during the second week of May 1994, she along with her daughter came to Bangalore via Trivandrum.

In Bangalore, Nasif stayed with Ali Nazir, son of Ibrahim Nazir, the former president of Maldives. For a brief period, Fauzia and her daughter stayed in the house of Ali Nazir. When Nasif left Bangalore, Fauzia searched for another accommodation. Wilkinson, a friend of Ali Nazir, helped her to locate a house. She took a portion of the house owned by Ms Sara Palani on rent and stayed there with her daughter.

Fauzia sought the assistance of Wilkinson for the admission of her daughter. First, they approached the principal of Bishop Cotton School who demanded ₹25,000 as donation for admission. This amount was paid to Wilkinson to finalize the admission, but the school authorities subsequently backed out and suggested to approach Baldwin School for the admission. The principal of that school demanded ₹50,000 for admission. As she had no money to meet this demand, she contacted her daughter Nasiha in Malé and requested to arrange at least US$1,500 for admission expenses. Nasiha arranged the money and tried to locate someone going to Bangalore, to send the amount.

Then Nasiha sought the help of Mariam who had visited Bangalore earlier and was familiar with the city. As planned, Mariam reached Bangalore airport on 20 June 1994. Fauzia along with her daughter Jila Hamdi was there to receive her. Mariam came out with a bearded man whom she introduced as Chandrasekharan. He offered to drop them in their place of stay. As Fauzia had engaged a prepaid taxi, they took the taxi, while he left the airport in his own car. On the way, Mariam handed over US$1,700 to Fauzia, while some gift packets sent by Nasiha were collected from the hotel where Mariam stayed.

Fauzia's Bangalore story was almost on the lines of the statement made by Mariam. The main characters were, of course, Chandrasekharan, Sharma and his friend. The thread of the story was running on the admission of Jila Hamdi. Mrs Thomas, the principal of the Baldwin School, her husband Thomas, etc., played minor roles.

Once the admission formalities of her daughter were over, she and Mariam returned to Malé in July 1994. During the last week of July, both of them left for Sri Lanka for different tasks: Fauzia to collect the school leaving certificate of her daughter from Colombo-based Belvoir College International and Mariam as a cover agent of NSS to meet Mohammed Mohsin, another Malé national working for NSS. Both the ladies stayed with Shanti Samarcone at Piliyandala, Colombo.

After a brief stay in Colombo, Mariam left for Bangalore. Her mission in Bangalore was the collection of details of Malé nationals working against the Maldivian president. Soon Fauzia also left for Bangalore to see her daughter. She carried an audio cassette given by Ahmed Manick, the director of Radio Maldives. The cassette contained some Hindi ghazals rendered into 'Divehi' language by Ms Mariam Saeed, Ali Nazir's mother.

On reaching Bangalore, she stayed with Ms Sara Palani and met Mariam and Jila. One day, she along with Mariam visited the house of Ali Nazir and handed over the cassette. On another occasion, she alone visited Ali Nazir and discussed about the formalities connected with the visa of her daughter Jila Hamdi. On his instructions, the photocopies of the passport and the letter from her school were arranged and delivered to him.

Then surfaced the episode of Dr Anand and the platonic role of Chandrasekharan! On Chandraskharan's assurance that he would soon arrange the blissful meeting between Mariam and Anand, the ladies returned to Trivandrum and stayed at Hotel Samrat. Before leaving Bangalore, they gave him their contact number in Trivandrum which was the number of Hotel Samrat.

Days were monotonous in Hotel Samrat where Fauzia felt lonely and depressed. Then, she came across her cousin Mohammed Naeem who was in Trivandrum in connection with the treatment of his mother and wife. Naeem and his family were staying at Geethanjali, a house owned by Maldivian national Ali Nazib. Along with Naeem's family members and other relatives, she went for a picnic to Neyyar Dam site near Trivandrum where photographs were taken.

While staying in Hotel Samrat, she made telephonic calls to Ms Sara Palani and Jila Hamdi in Bangalore, her daughter Nasiha and other relatives in Malé, Maldivian Airlines and PRS Hospital, Trivandrum, etc. She also received a call from Dr Sasikumaran which was meant for Mariam. One day, Sasikumaran came to the hotel with his wife and met Mariam. Fauzia did not meet them, but requested Mariam to talk to Sasikumaran whether he could help them in getting visa for Jila Hamdi. Later when Sasikumaran alone visited the hotel, Fauzia, after getting introduced by Mariam, discussed Jila's visa problem. He suggested her to meet home secretary and Bangalore police commissioner and explain the position; later, he would take up the matter with the home secretary.

The visa issue of Jila continued to haunt her. Meanwhile, Nasiha who reached Trivandrum en route to Bangalore informed that

Ali Nazir was unable to arrange her visa and she needed to visit Malé for getting visa. Then Fauzia got an opportunity to discuss the visa issue with Rameez, a Maldivian national who was staying in the same hotel in connection with treatment. As he promised to help her in getting the visa of Jila Hamdi with the help of his friend in Indian embassy, Malé, she arranged and delivered copies of passport and other documents to him. For that purpose, Sara Palani faxed the documents from a booth at Bangalore to the reception of Hotel Samrat.

But Rameez also could not help her in arranging the visa. Thus, Fauzia went to Bangalore to bring her daughter to Trivandrum for sending her to Malé to obtain her visa. Accordingly, she along with her daughter reached Trivandrum during the first week of October 1994. Jila Hamdi after staying a couple of days with her mother left for Malé. Though Fauzia and Mariam had also planned to go to Malé along with her, they could not make it due to non-availability of flight tickets. They had to wait indefinitely for the open tickets, especially as Indian Airlines cancelled their flights to Malé.

Meanwhile, validity of Mariam's visa was to expire on 14 October 1994. Both the ladies went to the police commissioner's office, Trivandrum, one day ahead to get her visa extended. Mariam explained her position to the officer in charge of the section. He asked to deposit her passport for processing the case for extension. Later, he visited Mariam in her room on the pretext of verifying her details. Later, the hotel reception staff was questioned and the hotel/telephone bills of the ladies were scrutinized. On verifying the telephone numbers contacted by them from the hotel, the name of Sasikumaran had come up. The ladies clarified that his (Sasikumaran) reference was given by Chandrasekharan of Bangalore.

For the next couple of days, both the ladies met the officer and requested to expedite the extension of Mariam's visa. For extension of Mariam's visa, she was asked to produce the air ticket confirming her departure to Malé. On 16 October 1994, when the ladies met the inspector with the confirmed ticket of Mariam, he asked Mariam to cancel the ticket and remain in the hotel. He seized her passport, while Fauzia was also asked to surrender her passport. As her passport was left in the hotel, she did not surrender it. The officer again questioned them regarding their contacts in Trivandrum and Bangalore and finally directed them not to contact Dr Sasikumaran who is not a medical professional, but a senior space scientist.

Later, officers in uniform and civil dress visited the hotel and questioned them and the hotel staff. This exercise continued for a couple of days. Meanwhile, on 19 October, Fauzia's daughter arrived at Trivandrum from Malé en route to Bangalore. Her school was already opened. Fauzia left for Bangalore along with her without informing the police.

In Bangalore, Fauzia was busy with the registration formalities of her daughter for which she visited commissioner's office. Then, a man in civil dress who claimed to be a police officer came to Sara Palani's house and discreetly collected more details about Fauzia. Ms Palani was thoroughly shaken by this exercise. Later, the aforementioned officer questioned Fauzia mainly about her connections with Sasikumaran and other scientists and her contacts with Pak officials in Malé. He mentioned many new names which she had never heard in her life.

This followed the visit of four other persons including the one who had already questioned her. They claimed to be officers from Delhi and recorded her statement regarding her stay and activities in India. Then two officers who claimed to be from Trivandrum and Bangalore came to her place and took her to Trivandrum. Thus, Fauzia with the officers landed at Trivandrum on 11 November 1994.

THE HONEY TRAPS AND HONEYBEES

4

The nodal officer of ISRO spy case at the state Bureau headquarters was impatient. With curious eyes, he came to me a couple of times and enquired about the progress of my task.

'Could you find something sensational? These ladies are hard nuts to crack, really trained and infiltrated by our enemies! You have to pick up contradictions in their statements and confront them. Then only, they will break and come out with all the truth.' The small man spoke like a seasoned detective who unravelled many sensational espionage cases!

I felt like laughing, but controlled my feelings and became serious. How quickly officers like him reach grave conclusions without any logic or basis. I felt perhaps he may be parroting the subjective impressions of his bosses. After all I couldn't find anything sensational in their statements except Mariam's personal escapades and her cover assignment with NSS of Maldives. But I kept my impressions guarded, while he went on using sexual innuendos for the accused women.

Thank God, his telephone started ringing and he reluctantly stopped the narration and rushed to his cabin.

I came out of the cabin and walked to the main corridor where I saw Mr Indran from Mumbai stepping out of the room of the senior boss. I had the opportunity to work under him when he was the second in command of the Kerala set-up. His assignment in Mumbai for the last couple of years has made him almost completely bald, fattier and pot-bellied. He immediately recognized me.

'Hello, all the old veterans are here! What are you trying to cook up?' His sarcastic words came out.

'No sir, nothing of that sort; I only landed today. I heard that you got everything from these ladies.' I took more liberties with my old boss and accompanied him through the corridor.

With my past background, the Delhi headquarters deputed me to question the ladies. I completed the task in a couple of days. Nothing startling or sensational from our point of view except that these ladies were helping the Malé secret service by furnishing inputs on the activities of anti-Gayoom elements based in Bangalore and Trivandrum. Their diaries in Malé language were deciphered and information to this effect was corroborated. But the press is coming out with all cock and bull stories out of nothing. Actually I am in a hurry to catch the Mumbai flight.'

He walked down the steps in hurry.

That was new information. While returning to the cabin, I wondered why the local bosses are making warlike preparations? Mr Indran's words echoed in my ears: What are you trying to cook up?

The nodal officer came running with excitement.

'Some of our veteran interrogators from Delhi have landed. They are interacting with our local boss. They will be soon proceeding to the reserve camp to further question the ladies. You can also join them. The vehicle is kept ready.' He went running to the room of the senior boss.

I went to his cabin and found Kumar as cool as ever, simply gossiping with his subordinates. A bunch of handwritten statements were scattered on his table. On seeing me, he became active and quick instructions were given to his assistant.

'You decipher this bunch of "waste" and prepare something for our boss. Don't be serious; whatever we put up, he will cut and size up according to his imagination. That is his style.' I felt that this fellow can never change. He will openly blame the seniors in front of his subordinates, but kneel before the bosses when he meets them!

I handed over the interrogation statements of the ladies to him and left the cabin. At the ground floor, the driver was impatiently waiting; a young fellow who was known to me for many years.

'Sir, I came to know that you have come. When are we going to the camp? You please help me to see the ladies', he seemed more courteous and obedient.

I felt how much sensation these people have created on the physical characteristics of these Maldivian ladies. What immediately flashed through my mind was the funny scene from a Malayalam movie: The key characters were young mischievous youths of a rural arts club. The occasion was its inauguration. They ingeniously worked out a plan to attract maximum crowd. Wide publicity was given that the chief guest would be none other than Silk Smitha, the sexy heart-throb of the young and old on the silver screen. The entire rural folk marched to the venue to get a glimpse of that heroine who ignites their emotions. There was total commotion at the venue. Organizers found it difficult to control the crowd. But the people were damn happy on getting a glance of that great actress. Finally, the cat was out of the bag. It was not Silk Smitha but only her dupe! Imagine the fate of the organizers!

What again struck my mind were Mr Indran's words. Genuine doubts came up. Is it a similar sort of drama like the aforementioned film scene? And if it is, then who is the director? What are his real intentions? I mused.

The script is ready with basic ingredients of a spy thriller. A Maldivian lady shuttling between India and Malé via Sri Lanka, bizarre episodes of this lady entranced by males having some resemblance of her school-time boyfriend, cover assignment of a lady for a secret service, the scientists of a sensitive space establishment in her honey trap, liaison man of foreign corporate house eager to help any beautiful lady in distress and, of course, dollar and Indian money aplenty. Key actors have also lined up: interrogators, analysts, technical team and specialists in counter-espionage operations and finally the big bosses! The only doubt was whether the drama would hit the box office or turn into a damp squib?

My thoughts were interrupted. Silk Smitha vanished from my mind. The image of Mariam reappeared. The vehicle with expert interrogators from Delhi speeded through the highway. A bespectacled gentleman with Mongoloid look broke the silence.

'I am Maru and this is my colleague Jitu. We belong to the IB's Delhi unit. We are new to this place and you will be of much help to us.' There was an air of confidence in his voice. The lean and tall Jitu, full of pimples on his face, was still silent.

Soon we reached the camp well guarded by armed sentries. The camp commandant had issued specific instructions not to allow anyone to meet the ladies without his permission. But we had no difficulty in getting inside. A local officer who had been loitering there since the arrest of the ladies had better liaison with the commandant and others there. Jitu was surprised on seeing him there. Both shared their past thrilling episodes and experiences in Delhi. How true is the saying that the birds of the same feather flock together! Soon, they had their own ways!

Both ladies were kept in separate rooms—Fauzia on the ground floor and Mariam on the first floor. Their security was provided by earmarked women police personnel on rotation under the supervision of one senior personnel, Elsa. She had a tough time as there was a beeline of police personnel and interrogators of different agencies to quiz Mariam. Elsa was really amazed at the steady flow of 'male honeybees' towards this 'queen bee' who apparently was weaving a honey trap!

Accompanied by a local guard, we went to Fauzia's room. A team of officers from different agencies were quizzing her. Another queue of officers was there waiting for its turn. A fragile looking Fauzia in her shabby dress and uncombed hair looked really weak and depressed. I calmly observed the drama. Maru went to interact with the police officer in uniform. Jitu straight away went to Mariam's room.

It was getting dark. The interrogation team on job continued its exercise. The officers were in no mood to allow others to step in. The police officer suggested that it would be better to resume the exercise on the next day.

Maru and I went to meet the other lady. A crowd of interrogators was already there. A few of them were sitting close to Mariam and chit-chatting with her.

Maru joined his colleagues from Delhi as their accommodation was arranged separately in the same guest house. I returned with the young driver who somehow managed to get a glimpse of Mariam. He was really excited and felt that she was a replica of Silk Smitha! He made an innocuous comment that the poor police officer should not be blamed for his mad infatuation with the lady who turned down his pleas.

Finally, we reached the city hotel where I stayed for the night. The comment of the driver again and again flashed through my mind: The image of a police officer whose unjust pleas were turned down by a lady in distress! Slowly, his image vanished and I plunged into sleep.

A CONFESSION VIDEO

5

I was still in the bed in the midst of some sweet dreams. The extension phone in the room continuously rang. I took the receiver; I heard the nodal officer's excited words:

'The Delhi people have hit the jackpot. The ladies have confessed and narrated the entire episode. Now the things are taking a new turn. There would be more arrest and interrogation. Come to the office at the earliest; we have a lot of things to do.'

Our nodal officer was found to be quite impatient. There was no time to ask something more about the developments.

I reached the office well in advance. He was alone in his cabin. None had turned up. I felt that no one had taken his instructions seriously. That was the problem with him. He is in the habit of making mountains out of moles. Thus, subordinates failed to identify the real mountains! But he seemed quite happy with the new developments.

'Yesterday, the interrogation and other exercises continued for the whole night. The ladies were kept together in one room and our team monitored their conversations. The tech fellows recorded their talks; but not a single word could be deciphered or properly heard. These fellows are always like that.'

He unleashed his venom against the technical personnel attached to the operation and continued:

'But the interrogators from Delhi are marvellous. They applied all the techniques. The ladies have become flat and broken. Fauzia was ready to confess; she only wanted that her daughter should not be hunted and hurt. Her confession was videotaped during the wee hours. Delhi was informed; Bengali Dada, the senior IPS officer in Delhi monitoring the case, is very happy on the new turn of events. The video is now with our local boss. We will replay and watch it when he comes.'

He concluded as if something great was achieved.

Meanwhile, the state chief heading the Bureau reached the office. His intercom buzzed; that was a call for the nodal officer. He left the cabin in a hurry. Left alone in the room, I wondered what magic the Delhi team played to break the ladies? I felt something fishy.

The local tech people made the arrangements to replay the video in a safe secluded room. The state chief along with the nodal officer came there. I felt that he had become skinny and skeletal over the last few months. Perhaps his chronic diabetes might have aggravated due to overstrain. In his conventional style, he murmured few words:

'This is for the first time we are getting a typical CI case. We definitely have limitations as to how to professionally proceed with it. Thus, officers and interrogation experts from Delhi would be assisting us from time to time. Our officers can learn a lot from them. Officers like you who have experience in the field of CI and interrogation are summoned from outstations to actively associate in the case.'

His veiled smile really surprised me.

He asked the tech person to play the video. It was a 10- to 20-minute long video containing the confession of Fauzia. The image of a highly bewildered and frightened Fauzia appeared on the screen. In her choked voice, she narrated the whole story: her association with foreign intelligence agencies along with Mariam, tasks assigned to them, their visit to Trivandrum and Bangalore on various occasions, their handlers in Malé and Colombo, money and dollar received from handlers and handed over to Indian contacts like

Chandrasekharan and Dr Sasikumaran and relations with space scientists, etc.

The entire narration appeared like a filmy dialogue, prompted by somebody. The lady just like a novice playback singer frequently looked on both sides as if waiting for instructions. Sometimes, she had to keep wearing spectacles to read certain names from a piece of paper. Yet the names of other accused were not properly mentioned. I frankly expressed these observations. A visibly annoyed and embarrassed state chief shouted:

'What you think of yourself? You needn't conduct a post-mortem of the video or its contents. You should admit that Delhi people are professionally much superior to us in such matters. Even the senior bosses in Delhi have appreciated their work.'

He left the room in hurry.

I was fully convinced of the grounds of my doubts. It was not the first time that I faced such drubbing for speaking truth. But my stand was vindicated in due course. But the tragedy was that the senior bosses never admitted their Himalayan blunders. They always managed to make some others as scapegoats and came out unscathed from serious professional lapses.

The nodal officer's cabin became the main centre of activity. Additional manpower and resources poured in. Kumar appeared happy with more subordinates. He gave sermons to them and leisurely passed the time gossiping and blaming others.

Elated by their serious assignments, a new set of personnel were found to get busier: they contacted district units and directed the identified officers to join the interrogation teams, constituted interrogation teams, arranged transport and accommodation for outstation officers, deployed vehicles and drivers for operations, and last but not least liaised with the senior bosses from Delhi.

I was surprised to see how unprofessional the police and intelligence organizations were in sensitive assignments like interrogation. The fundamentals of this powerful tradecraft mechanism in the investigation of any kind of crime or offence were simply flouted. Personnel with basic qualities, professional background, relevant knowledge and experience in relation to the accused to be interrogated were never selected. Definitely, there was dearth of such trained personnel, but such deficiencies were covered up through shortcuts or gimmicks. Seldom had there been any proper planning, preparation and briefing of the officers on task! They acted on their own, always bullied, humiliated and tortured the victims during the process!

Past memories took me to the turbulent years that I spent in the north-eastern state of Assam: the AK Series gun-toting ultras openly roamed in the Brahmaputra Valley, cold-blooded killings, kidnapping and extortions and a helpless administration remaining as silent spectators. Then Operation Bajrang was launched with a big bang during the early 1990s. A massive counter-insurgency operation participated by army, central paramilitary forces (CPMF), state police and security/intelligence agencies! Senior bosses, who won Padma awards for their distinguished career in the Indian Police Service (IPS) and later elevated to gubernatorial assignments in sensitive states, had decisive roles in the entire operation.

However, the untold truth remained that not a useful piece of actionable intelligence could be generated through this exercise. Suspected ultras were detained from every nook and corner of the state. Their interrogation and collection of actionable intelligence was an integral part of the operation. Every Tom, Dick and Harry in the Bureau who worked in the north-east decades ago and never heard of the insurgent outfits like the United Liberation Front of Assam (ULFA) landed en masse from different parts of the country by air! Huge amounts were wasted from national exchequer. They were let loose to different destinations without proper planning or briefing. After a leisurely picnic, they returned empty-handed even without properly recording the personal particulars of the arrested.

Its echoes were heard during the joint coordination meeting of the top brass of various agencies when the army counterpart made unsavoury comments on the lack of ground-level intelligence. The intelligence/security bosses had to eat the humble pie. Yet they had not learnt the lessons. The end of the story was that Bajrang had been a total flop.

'Hi, Richard, what are you daydreaming? Don't get upset by the words of our state chief. After all he is under considerable stress and strain due to the continuous pressure from our bosses in Delhi. They want everything at the finger tips so that they can pass the buck easily to the higher formations.'

The words of the nodal officer had broken the chain of my memories.

Hectic activities continued in nodal officer's cabin: constituting and reconstituting interrogation teams. Some guys showed suspicious eagerness to get included in the team for interrogating Mariam, but they were quieted by the nodal officer.

Soon came my turn. I along with Maru and another local officer should confront Fauzia and Mariam. After all, we had seen and heard the confessional video of Fauzia based on which we can further interrogate the lady to get more specific details!

The reserve camp remained more alive: vehicles with beaconed lights moved here and there, and more and more new faces appeared at the main entrance. Ms Elsa with a blushed face welcomed us. We went directly to the room where Fauzia was kept. There was dead silence.

The super-sleuth SM of Kerala Police had already taken over the investigation. Officers of his cracking team were quizzing Fauzia. SM was closely monitoring them. I felt that over the years, he had not changed much. The same tall guy with engorged face and drooping eyes exhibiting all the features of an introvert.

We went nearer to him and extended all courtesy that an IPS officer deserved. With his typical style, he half opened his mouth. Inaudible half broken words came out:

'I have just taken over the investigation of the case as desired by senior bosses. I definitely need some time to properly understand the intricacies of the case. Meanwhile, I had a meeting with your state chief who told me that you are in the interrogation team.'

Slowly, he walked to the corner of the room as if he wanted to discuss something personal.

'What are your findings? Your Delhi people might have something more?' He seemed inquisitive.

'As far as my information goes, it is an NSS operation. Mr Indran from Mumbai who quizzed the ladies has such findings.' I revealed whatever I had gathered from others.

'What interest our NSS fellows have in Maldives?' There was much surprise on his face.

But this time, I was really stunned without knowing whether he was just joking or serious in his comments. However, I tried to clarify: 'Sir, not our NSS, the community outfit which is powerful in the Central Travancore of Kerala, what I mean is the NSS of Maldives.' I saw a blushed and embarrassed SM who left the spot without uttering a single word. I felt that his IPS ego was severely wounded.

SM was in a hurry to leave the place as if something explosive is on the offing. His cracking team also accompanied him. Maru joined the other members still quizzing Fauzia. I curiously watched the entire exercise as if a novice to the field. There was nothing niche in her revelations; only parroting of what she had stated in the video. Maru tried to create an impression that the plight of her daughter would be awful had she not come out with all truth. Her spontaneous reaction came: 'I parroted everything that you people have suggested on an assurance that nothing will happen to my daughter. Everything was videographed also. Then why this threat? If you want something more, I am ready to repeat.' There was sullen silence. The cat was out of the bag. Maru was really in an awkward situation. The compounder turned interrogator from Delhi suddenly intervened.

'You, bloody bitch, you need not explain what happened yesterday. Sir wanted to know what all things you have done.' His yelling echoed in the room. The frightened fragile Fauzia fumbled and fainted.

I felt there was no need to watch this drama. I withdrew to the corner of the room. Suddenly, a visibly agitated young officer, waiting for long to join the quizzing of the lady, came to me and started ventilating all his fury and frustration.

'I know you are also from the local Bureau; you people have hijacked the entire thing. Even the police personnel who detected the case were not allowed to question the suspects. For the last couple of days, I was trying to meet the ladies to clarify certain crucial points, but in vain. After all, with our foreign network, we are better placed in ascertaining many things.'

He stopped for a moment and took out a cigar.

Without any introduction, I understood that guy belonged to external intelligence wing. Poor guy, he was really worried as how could he face his boss without getting at least some tips about this sensational spy case! Really, he was going to unleash his deep frustration by smoking a cheap Charminar!

I could well imagine his predicament. After all, interrogation is a joint exercise by personnel belonging to different agencies. Then why this guy is not getting the opportunity? What came to his mind was the controversial video and spontaneous response of Fauzia. Things were getting clear in my mind, but there was none to share my thoughts. Everyone in the Bureau was in high spirits in bursting a spy network!

Soon the message reached. Rush to Kairali Latex Guest House located at the heart of the capital city. Through the humpy-bumpy road, the Bureau vehicle went ahead. Maru was silent all along. I broke his silence.

'What is your initial assessment?'

Through the thick power glass, Maru, the professional interrogator of the Bureau from Delhi, made a guarded look and said, 'Really a tough lady, who hides many secrets!'

I felt something strange; he too wanted to hide his true impressions and fall in line with the findings of the senior bosses monitoring the case! But soon I was convinced that birds of the same feather would definitely flock together, especially those from Delhi.

THE BEARDED MAN WITH SPARKLING EYES

6

The huge iron gate in front of the Kairali Latex Guest House opened with cracking sound. The Bureau vehicle with team members directly went inside the spacious compound. The driver who visited the place many times led us to the Guest House building.

Many new faces were hanging around the ground floor, corridors and steps leading to the first floor. A couple of canteen boys from the ground floor kitchen appeared near the main entrance and suddenly vanished. Everyone there was in a sense of surprise and anxiety.

Kumar with a couple of his subordinates was on the first floor. He broke the news that SM's team had already arrested Chandrasekharan of Bangalore and Sasikumaran, the space scientist. Chandrasekharan would be brought to the Guest House at any time for interrogation, whereas the interrogation of Sasikumaran had already been started at the Special Police camp.

The techies from Delhi were on the job to convert a spacious suite in the Guest House into an interrogation room. The bespectacled Bharat, the leader of the team, had wordy quarrel with others on every simple issue. Inside the room, they were fighting with each other to decide the seating arrangement of the suspect so that the entire interrogation can be clandestinely videographed from the adjacent room. Time was really running short. They placed and replaced the concealed camera at different spots and tested the clarity of the images. Finally, Maru intervened and sorted out the issue.

When the police vehicle entered the compound, more and more faces appeared at the corridors and windows to have a glimpse of the fellow who betrayed the nation on being entangled in the honey trap of two ladies! Irony was that people reached hasty conclusions based on what they see and read in the visual and the print media. A common man in the street is not to be blamed as he seldom ponders over such issues beyond what he gathers from the media.

Accompanied by half a dozen police personnel, he was taken to the first floor. Bewildered and panic-stricken, he stood like a statue in the midst of police personnel and the interrogators. With thick black beard and long uncombed hair, he exactly fit into the description given by the ladies in their statement. I was convinced that he was none but Chandrasekharan.

Soon the Guest House was virtually taken over by police and IB sleuths. More and more interrogators, techies and their supporting staff and the liaison personnel of various agencies poured in. The poor canteen staff of the Guest House had a tough time to satisfy these sleuths with different tasty cuisines. While the 'Bangla Babus' were mad after Pomfret, prawns and seer fish, the guys from Delhi had special craze for chicken and mutton!

Dalby, a senior IPS officer, and his subservient subordinate Singh from Delhi were the first to question Chandrasekharan. On their bullying and barking orders, he had to undress himself, leaving only his underpants! Obviously, a tactic usually adopted by all interrogators to size up the suspect. As both the officers were in a hurry, they had parroted that the Maldivian ladies had confessed everything, and thus Chandrasekharan had no option but to admit his involvement in the espionage network. They left the questioning halfway with a harsh warning that he should reveal everything to other interrogators.

I along with interrogators from Delhi took up the next phase of his interrogation. The story narrated by Chandrasekharan was really thrilling:

'I was born and brought up at a small town, North Paravur of Ernakulam district in Kerala. After my initial schooling at my native place, I joined for pre-university course (PUC) in UC College, Alwaye, but failed. Then I joined polytechnic in Thrissur, Kerala, from where I passed a Diploma in Mechanical Engineering in 1959. During the next 18 years, I took up more than half a dozen jobs in the areas of teaching, sales and marketing, and extensively travelled in all the four southern states. Beginning in 1977, I started taking up agencies of different firms based in Bombay, Baroda, Bangalore and Hyderabad.

My association with Mumbai-based M/S Seva Enterprises was a turning point in my life. The firm was one of the leading importers of machine tools from USSR to India. My job in Seva Enterprises enabled me to pick up Russian language and to establish contacts with Soviet officials who used to visit India. As their agent, I also looked after the visit of USSR trade representatives to Madras and Bangalore.

In 1984, I floated a proprietary concern, namely Vijay Industrial Consultants, with its main office in Bangalore. In 1991, we had become the Indian consultants of the Moscow-based firm M/S GK. The firm in 1990 signed an agreement with ISRO for the supply of cryogenic engines. As a representative of GK, our main function was to arrange travel and accommodation arrangements for the Russian delegation during their visit to ISRO establishments in Bangalore, Trivandrum, etc. We were paid an annual commission of ₹8 lakh for such services.

In 1994, GK appointed me as its representative for Middle East and Far East. In the same year, Vijay Industrial Consultants entered into an agreement with another Moscow-based company Technomash which was the supplier of machines and devices for ISRO's cryogenic engine project. As per the agreement, the

Technomash was to pay an annual commission of US$100,000 to our firm.

As representative of GK, I visited Russia many times, besides Singapore, Dubai, Colombo and the Middle East. During such visits to Moscow, I got opportunities to establish contact with a number of senior scientists of ISRO such as Dr Sasikumaran, Dr Nambi Narayanan, Vasudevan Gnana Gandhi and so on, who were on official visit to Russia under the ISRO–GK joint programme for working out subcontracting formalities.

During such visits, I also explored the possibility of starting new ventures in partnership with ISRO scientists, non-resident Indians (NRI) and Russians associated with GK and other companies. The 'Glasnost' and 'Perestroika', and internal issues in Soviet Union, gave vast opportunities for new entrepreneurs and investors for such endeavours. I took major initiative in 1995 to float a private firm to promote the commercial launching of satellites for countries interested in such ventures. The other partners of the proposed venture were Dr Muthunayakam and Sasikumaran (of ISRO), Alexi Vasin (GK) and Anthony Varghese (NRI/Singapore). I was also in touch with Thomas Kurisingal of Cochin, the representative of Amada&Shultz, USA, for canvassing orders from other countries for satellite launching. Thomas was confident of arranging orders from Sri Lanka provided that Ms Chandrika Kumaratunga becomes the prime minister (PM) there. However, the plan to float the company misfired as Dr Muthunayakam backed out from the project.

Using my close connections with Thomas Kurisingal, I tried to arrange a loan of US$500 million through a consortium of banks in the USA and the Middle East to a firm called AIGEO MDB Aviation Ltd, Moscow, in which I was an honorary director. Thomas was offered 4 per cent commission in this transaction. I came into contact with Dr Brooks, the managing director of this company, through the chairman of GK. Dr Brooks' firm had subsequently entered into an agreement with Hindustan Aeronautics Limited (HAL), Bangalore, for the manufacture of small aircraft.

As per the agreement, two prototypes were to be supplied to Moscow firm before 1995. Dr Brooks also visited Bangalore during the first week of August 1994.

I also explored the possibility of working out an agreement with the HAL for the procurement of sophisticated machines and technology. This move was made at the insistence of one Mahadevan of M/S Manav Consultants, Bangalore, who participated in a machine tool exhibition in Germany in 1993 where latest equipment/machinery was displayed. However, I could not go ahead with the proposal as the HAL showed lukewarm response.

In the wake of GK, getting licence for the export of spare parts of Russian-made equipment–machines to other countries, I, through my representative in Delhi, tried to get registration for the supply of spare parts to defence establishments in India. The details of defence ministry officials in charge of such matters were collected and forwarded to GK. However, the deal could not be struck with the defence ministry due to technical issues.

On many occasions, I tried to help a few ISRO scientists/officials to get cleared the inflated tenders for the procurement of machines/equipment from Russian firms such as GK, Technomash and Forbes, etc. In June 1993, on behalf of these scientists/officials, I negotiated with the representatives of some of these firms in respect of the supply of items such as rotary vacuum furnace, EB welding with single gum and twin gum, pocket mill machine, etc., which cost many crores. Some of these equipment and machines were vital for the manufacture of ISRO's cryogenic and Vikas Engine projects.'

It is quite natural to suspect his involvement in the espionage case especially in the light of his background, close links with Russian firms having agreement with ISRO in the manufacture of cryogenic engines and the suspected deals with defence establishments. The interrogators especially those guided by the senior bosses from Delhi, to a great extent, were misled by his disclosures. Chandrasekharan under considerable pressure and intimidation by some overbearing interrogators could present a convincing story with many characters and places that fully fit into the theory of espionage.

'My first meeting with Mariam Rasheeda was quite accidental when the lady was pleading with Indian Airlines staff of the Trivandrum Airport to get her air ticket confirmed for the journey from Trivandrum to Bangalore on 20 June 1994. She had some problems with the Air Customs people in the airport. I was also a traveller of the same flight. A foreign lady at an unknown land; I came to her help and successfully pleaded with the counter staff to ok the ticket. Mariam got her ticket confirmed and thanked me for the timely help. She had noted down my Bangalore telephone number. On reaching Bangalore airport, I offered her lift up to her place of stay, but she declined it, as her friend was there to receive her.

The next day, I got a telephone call from Mariam. This time, she sought my help for the admission of her friend's daughter in a good school in Bangalore. Naturally, I invited her and her friend, Ms Fauzia, to Windsor Manor Hotel, Bangalore, where they were offered breakfast. Then they came to my office. Fauzia narrated her woes regarding the admission of her daughter in Baldwin School, Bangalore, for which she had not enough money to make donation, etc. V. T. Thomas, husband of the vice principal of the school, was known to me. As he was staying at Indira Nagar, far away from my office, I decided to seek the help of my friend S. K. Sharma who also knew Thomas. Meanwhile, on the request of Fauzia, I made arrangements to get exchanged US$1,000 into Indian currency.

They again visited me at my office during September 1994 before their scheduled departure to Malé via Trivandrum. During conversation, Mariam sought my assistance for her medical check-up for heart ailments in the newly established Manipal Hospital, near Airport, Bangalore. As I had no known contacts there, I referred the name of D. Sasikumaran, the senior scientist of ISRO, Trivandrum, whose wife is an assistant professor in the Medical College, Trivandrum. I gave Mariam the telephone number of Sasikumaran.

While discussing about her medical check-up, etc., the name of Dr Anand Saldanha of Mangalore came up and both the ladies started quarrelling with each other in their own tongue. When enquired about the issue, Mariam disclosed that she was in love with the doctor whom she intended to marry soon. She for the first time met the doctor at the rented apartment of Ms Fauzia in Bangalore. However, Fauzia was not in favour of their affair. Later, Mariam lost contact with the doctor. When she pleaded to me to help her establishing contact with Dr Saldanha, Fauzia walked out of my room in fits of anger. I promised to help her. Before leaving the room, I assured her to contact the doctor soon.

Later, I came to know from Sasikumaran that the ladies on reaching Trivandrum checked in Hotel Samrat. Mariam contacted Sasikumaran, who in turn informed me that he was in touch with the ladies. Subsequently, I came to know about their arrest first from Sasikumaran and later from my friends in Trivandrum.'

During day and night, teams of interrogators had come and gone: some serious, others overenthusiastic with the sole aim to break the suspect by hook or crook, yet some others lethargic and indifferent and last but not least those who were committed to fabricate an espionage story. In their midst, thoroughly shaken by anxiety, tension and exhaustion, Chandrasekharan who showed the signs of chest pain was taken to the nearby hospital for medical check-up. The doctor in the casualty diagnosed his symptom due to over anxiety and tension. It was a relief that his ECG was normal and other parameters stable.

I felt that Chandrasekharan has both physical and cerebral skills to overcome pressing situations. His early struggling life, taking up over half a dozen jobs, as sales representative, marketing executive and small-scale entrepreneur helped him to develop such qualities. His past experience in various fields, a chain of well-placed contacts and acquaintance with people holding senior positions in various sectors facilitated him to weave convincing stories. At times, he could convince his stand through such stories or claims that appeared to be true or real. In order to extract more out of such stories, some interrogators posed leading questions that enabled him to expand his stories on true espionage lines. Thus, the dividing line between the facts and fiction, truth and untruth and semi-truths and typical lies in his disclosures was so thin that the interrogators were unable to vouch their veracity. Through such tactics, he, to a great extent, could avoid the intimidation, humiliation and threat of torture by some of the interrogators. Thus, he continued his espionage story:

'The plot to sell the sensitive information pertaining to the flight details of Polar Satellite Launch Vehicle (PSLV) of ISRO was hatched during September 1993 when I along with Sasikumaran decided to make some quick money by selling secret information relating to space technology to interested parties. The inspiration for the same came to our mind when Alexi Vasin of GK confided to us that Dr Nambi Narayanan, the senior scientist of ISRO who had technical and other information on cryogenic engines and related projects, secretly passed such information to various foreign agencies and space establishments on payment.

Accordingly, during the first week of December 1993, I visited Trivandrum and stayed in Hotel Fort Manor along with a Russian delegation of GK. Dr Nambi Narayanan, who used to liaise with such delegations to discuss project details, was also staying in the same hotel. I incidentally met Fauzia along with a minor girl in the room of Nambi Narayanan. Later, over a couple of pegs of drinks, Nambi casually revealed that the aforementioned lady is a Maldivian national with high connections.

[This was a typical example of how Chandrasekharan wove stories mixing up truths and typical lies. It was true that Nambi Narayanan used to liaise with visiting Russian delegations; the statement such as that he had seen Fauzia with a minor girl in Nambi's room was totally fabricated. He wanted to involve Nambi Narayanan in the case and thereby to please some interrogators. Even the Hotel Fort Manor which he refers to was not operational at that time; then the question doesn't arise regarding the presence of Fauzia in the hotel along with a minor girl.]

Thus, I decided to cultivate this lady for our espionage operation. After detailed conversation with the lady, I offered to provide sensitive information on PSLV flight details. Fauzia did not make any commitment. However, she had not declined the offer, but conveyed that she would let me know the decision after sometime. Again, during the last week of December 1993, I and the Russian delegation stayed in the same hotel where Fauzia turned up with happy news. Her boss had agreed for the deal, by which all the sensitive details pertaining to PSLV should be provided by 15 October 1994; an amount of US$45,000 would be paid in three instalments. Sasikumaran was kept abreast of all the developments.

During the third week of January 1994, I, Fauzia and Sasikumaran met in Madras International Hotel for the transaction. Fauzia handed over two separate envelopes containing US$10,000 and 5,000 each to Sasikumaran and me, respectively, whereas Sasikumaran handed over a big envelope containing PSLV flight details to Fauzia. On coming out of the hotel, her envelope was collected by Zuhavardhi, an Indian Muslim. Immediately after the departure of Fauzia, two other persons, namely Zaukat and Mohammed Khaleel, who were from Thousand Lights Mosque area met Sasi and me in the hotel and informed that next payment would be made in June and by that time the required information should be ready.'

That was a convincing espionage story presented by Chandrasekharan which needed a lot of probe to ascertain its veracity. Thus, our team decided to urgently submit these details to the state Bureau headquarters with our specific comments. Meanwhile, another team of interrogators comprising local Bureau officers reported for the next phase of interrogation during late hours. We confided to them the details of the claims and disclosures made by Chandrasekharan and cautioned that leading questions based on media reports or other rumours may not be put to him as he is an expert in weaving convincing statements out of such inputs. The leader of the team who used to boast on his success in unearthing spy rings in the border areas of the country and running a network of potential agents for CI operations was least interested in such briefing. His stand was that he knew well how to tackle the suspect.

Back to the state Bureau headquarters, I went straight to the room of the nodal officer who was closeted by a group of officers and staff of the local office and interrogators and techies from Delhi. Some among them were eager to get some spicy piece of information which they wanted to share with their media or political contacts. Kumar was struggling with a bunch of papers to draft a report on the disclosures made by other suspects during questioning.

'Richard, we learnt that your team was successful in breaking Chandrasekharan who started spilling the beans. His sensitive disclosures will further strengthen our case. You draft the report immediately as our boss wanted to communicate the same to Delhi at the earliest.' The nodal officer was tense and impatient.

'Sir, yes, he has started talking, but I feel that many of his disclosures are mere cock and bull stories to escape from the heat of interrogation. How can we send such stories to Delhi without verification?' I clarified the position.

'Not at all. Our state chief has cleared that all such disclosures would be promptly communicated to our senior bosses in Delhi with specific comments. Let them decide the immediate course of action. No doubt, we will verify the disclosures pertaining to our area and promptly communicate the rest with other Bureaus to get their immediate feedback.'

He was little bit agitated over my stand.

I felt certain that any further argument on the matter will not serve any purpose as the state chief has preconceived notions and convictions. I withdrew to the corner of the room and started scribbling the report.

His room was still overcrowded with every Tom, Dick and Harry. I wondered how meekly he compromised with the basic canons of restrictive security, especially in the case of a sensitive spy case. Such gossips and loose talks based on media write-ups continued. Some were eager to know how that blue-eyed IPS officer of the state CM whose name was mentioned in some vernacular dailies was entangled in the honey trap? While some others tried to unfold the past stories to substantiate his involvement, I heard heated arguments made by some of the local officers and staff against the powerful political leader allegedly defending him in the entire episode!

The nodal officer just like the quiz master of a thrilling quiz competition was found occasionally sharing clues on the other possible characters of the spy drama who were catalogued by the sleuths of the Bureau with the help of old records and network of informers among the resident Maldivians of the state capital and the Sri Lankans or Maldivians shuttling between Sri Lanka and Kerala. A couple of such sleuths had hectic time to brief and debrief such potential informers to collect more specific inputs for confronting the suspects! Ironically, they also tried in vain to undertake a swift visit to Maldives and Sri Lanka on the pretext of tracing the tentacles of espionage network!

Many questions came to my mind. How erratically the responsible law enforcement and intelligence officers ordained to work for the security of the nation and safety of people behave and get influenced by the gossips and fancied stories of media? How the names of innocent and reputed persons are linked to the so-called spy case? What are their actual motives and designs? It has become easy to find the answers when the spy story has started to unfold at different levels.

7
THE BEARDED MAN WEAVES NEW CHARACTERS

The next day when our team resumed the interrogation of Chandrasekharan, he was in a rebellious mood. On seeing his swollen cheeks partially blue but covered with beard, I could easily guess the reason for his belligerence. I tried to lighten the situation.

'I think you had no proper sleep yesterday? If you are still feeling sleepy, we will start our exercise after some time.'

I consciously put the bait before him to know his response.

'I know your game better. What to talk of sleep in the midst of humiliating torture by your people?' He seemed to be hostile.

I was really in dilemma. Should I let down our interrogators to boost up his morale? How to tame a hostile Chandrasekharan and motivate him to speak?

'Perhaps you have not cooperated with our interrogators? Isn't it?' With an innocent smile, I pleaded.

'How can I swallow their stories full of lies? Finally I was exhausted.' I saw a mischievous smile on his bearded face.

'Forget yesterday's ordeal. You have to narrate how you were trapped into the net.' It was the turn of my co-interrogator.

I closely watched his reaction. I saw clear signals on his face to open his mind.

'Then we can go back to Madras International where we last stopped. What all happened there?' Another interrogator bluntly put the question.

His sparkling eyes extended, Adam's apple rhythmically expanded and contracted, and the face muscles strained and manifested the signs of excitement and anxiety, clearly indicating that he was going to fabricate something for our consumption. Yet we heard it patiently.

'When our transaction was over, "Coatvala" who was also known as Brigadier along with a Madras-based Kerala businessman close to Sasikumaran came to the hotel. I saw the Coatvala who is a senior officer of Kerala Police for the first time. Sasikumaran disclosed to me that Coatvala's main role is to give protection to our activities and transactions, for which some consideration and facilities were given to him. He has well-placed contacts and friends in a number of defence establishments and research organizations in Karnataka, Tamil Nadu, Andhra Pradesh and Kerala. He was present during our meeting in Indira Nagar, Bangalore, in September 1994. The meeting was meant to discuss and finalize certain transactions with Zuhaira, a Maldivian lady having business in India, Maldives and Sri Lanka. Besides Zuhaira, others who attended the secret meeting were Sasikumaran, S. K. Sharma, Fauzia and Mariam.'

Chandrasekharan continued his story closely watching our reaction. We also decided to patiently hear the story.

'Coatvala was also interested to launch certain business ventures along with Sasikumaran and me. One such venture was "Cavalier Project" for the manufacture of bulletproof vests. Coatvala assured us that he would find market for the product in Kerala Police and other defence establishments. This project was only in formative stage. Another project for which some initial discussions were held among us was "Carbon–Carbon Composite", a unit for the manufacture of high-temperature resistant, special light material which is used in aircraft, satellite, etc. Some of the bulk consumers of such products were ISRO, HAL and Taneja Airways.'

We could take his story with a pinch of salt. After all, since the arrest of the Maldivian ladies, the media were flooded with all speculative stories centring on a senior police officer. Thus, we had gone into the minute details of his disclosure on Coatvala, pointing out the contradictions and conflicts. When confronted, he claimed that initially the Coatvala was known in their circles as Brigadier as he always dressed in the manner of a senior army officer. On further clarification as why he was nicknamed as Coatvala, Chandrasekharan held that even in summer he appeared wearing coats, which was perhaps his weakness. On further questioning as how he could vouch that the person nicknamed as Brigadier and Coatvala is one and the same and identical with the IPS officer, allegedly linked to the espionage network, he took the stand that he heard the same from others including some interrogators. Thus, it was clear that some interrogators based on media reports would have posed leading question to him about the involvement of this IPS officer, which enabled him to come out with this detailed story.

We were surprised when SM with his crack team entered the interrogation room. Being a senior IPS officer in charge of the investigation of the case, I got up from the seat and welcomed SM and his team. A visibly bewildered Chandrasekharan also stood up with folded hands.

'Why you wretched fellow is staring at me? You sit down and tell the truth.' SM's disgusting words made Chandrasekharan more nervous. He turned towards his crack team and murmured: 'You continue the questioning of this fellow and record everything. I shall join you after a couple of minutes.' SM nodded at me to accompany him to the corner of the room.

'You see, I had an urgent call from your state chief. According to him, Sasikumaran has confessed to the interrogators that Fauzia and others were in constant touch with the controversial IPS officer. I had been to the interrogation place where he is still interrogated by your people. Just now, I got the information that this fellow had also confessed on the same lines. The picture is now almost clear.'

I saw a mischievous smile on his face.

'Sir, Chandrasekharan has come out with such a story in which the controversial officer was known in their circles as Coatvala or Brigadier and never spelt out the name of Raman Srivastava. But his version is full of contradictions and needs more corroboration and clarity.'

I put our findings across him.

'We cannot just brush aside the disclosures of this fellow. Perhaps, you may not be aware that this Coatvala is not a saint in our circles. Definitely he has known vices and weaknesses. Naturally, his past has started haunting him now. But as his colleague in the same force, my question is "to be or not to be". Now, really I am in a catch-22 situation.'

SM tried to present himself as a God-fearing upright officer fully committed to truth.

He joined his crack team and questioned Chandrasekharan for about half an hour. His questions were mainly on his financial transactions, his actual role in GK, his links with Sasi, Mariam, Fauzia and Coatvala, etc. Chandrasekharan repeated all what he had disclosed to us and other interrogation teams.

SM, after his brief interrogation, had informal interaction with the interrogators and investigators on the next course of action. He was of the view that the best method to establish truth is to confront him with other suspects and to clarify crucial points of differences and contradictions. Everyone endorsed his suggestion.

The venue of the drama was shifted to a spacious hall on the ground floor of the guest house. Special seating arrangements were made for the suspects and interrogators. More and more police personnel, interrogators and techies representing different agencies poured in. The star of attraction was SM, who over the years had established a prominent niche in the field of criminal investigations in Kerala. The sleuths of local Bureau including our nodal officer were present to witness the drama.

The young sleuths were a little disappointed when they came to know that Mariam would not be brought for this exercise. The fragile shabbily dressed Fauzia accompanied by a couple of women police personnel was brought in. Then it was the turn of Chandrasekharan who, despite sleepless nights and arduous questioning for days, tried to present a brave face.

Finally, the curtain was raised. Interrogators shot a volley of questions pertaining to the venue of the meeting of the suspects and agents for transactions, persons present, financial transactions and payments. SM posed two to three specific questions on the presence or otherwise of Coatvala in Madras and Bangalore and the confusion cantering around his name as revealed by Fauzia and Chandrasekharan and, of course, his identity features.

While Chandrasekharan tried to stick on to his version, Fauzia was confused on many issues. There were moments of anger and frustration on the part of Fauzia when Chandrasekharan flatly condemned her for her disclosures on the payments made to him at different places. In fact, the exercise instead of throwing more lights on the secret meetings and the participants thereof created more confusion. SM left the place in a hurry giving specific instructions to the members of his crack team.

Meanwhile, another exercise was on to identify the photograph of Coatvala from among half a dozen photographs of different persons having almost identical features. These photos were cut from various vernacular dailies. Of course, the initiative was taken by the interrogators from Delhi assisted by a couple of local sleuths bent upon implicating the Coatvala in the spy scandal. They had shown these photos to Fauzia for identification. In the presence of interrogators, police personnel and techies, the bewildered lady on a spur of moment identified the original photo of Coatvala as if the parrot of a juggler lady picking up the desired card from a packet of cards embedded amidst the glossy pictures of gods and goddesses.

The next day when I was going through the vernacular dailies, I was really shocked on the manner how they brought out cover stories focusing on the involvement of IGP Raman Srivastava in the espionage case. Some of these dailies had given detailed accounts as how Fauzia identified his photograph in the presence of senior officers representing various agencies. A couple of dailies had even highlighted his code names such as Coatvala or Brigadier. Certain big sharks were definitely after him!

Even Chandrasekharan was found in a lighter vein. Somehow he had also come to know about the turn of events. When we continued the interrogation, Chandrasekharan presented before us more and more characters and episodes, and repeated the disclosures made to different teams of interrogators.

One such fascinating character was Zuhaira, whose name had been in the records of various agencies as a key player in Malé-based espionage or anti-Indian activities by Pakistan. Initially, through indirect questioning we tried to ascertain whether he had come across any such name. His answer always was an emphatic 'no'. Subsequently, when he disclosed about the presence of this lady in Indira Nagar (Bangalore) meeting in which Coatvala was present, I was fully convinced of the real intentions of some of the interrogators! Yet we were patient enough to hear Chandrasekharan's story.

'I, for the first time, met Zuhaira, Maldivian lady settled in Colombo, in Taj Gateway Hotel, Bangalore, during the third week of March 1993. Initially, I picked up conversation with her in the hotel lobby and came to know that she had business interests in Colombo. As she used to visit the hotel on weekends, I could develop further friendship with her. During that period, she was staying at Vasant Vihar area. Later, I made a proposal to her to start a joint venture on computer products in Sri Lanka. She promised to discuss the proposal with her family and left for Colombo in April 1993.

On her return to India, I met her in the same hotel during August 1993. She intimated that her family was not interested in computer business. However, our friendship and intimacy developed further into consensual sex. In November 1993, Zuhaira made a proposal that she was interested in getting sensitive information on defence and scientific establishments such as ISRO, HAL, Gas Turbine Research Institute and Air Defence Establishment (ADE), located in Bangalore. On an assurance that I would provide such information on payment, she intimated that her Boss Mehboob Pasha would visit Trivandrum during December 1993 to discuss the details and finalize the deal.'

When I heard the name of Mehboob Pasha, I was doubly sure somebody had tutored Chandrasekharan a story that they wanted to hear from him. Just like Zuhaira, this Pasha had also prominently figured in the informer reports of some of these agencies in different pseudonyms such as Mohammed Pasha or Mazar Khan, as a high level Pak agent operating from Colombo. To my utter surprise, Chandrasekharan repeated these names a couple of times and finally stuck on to Mehboob Pasha for building up an exciting story.

'Mehboob Pasha, the Pakistani businessman based in Colombo, engaged in the export of tea, coffee, pepper, etc., from Sri Lanka to Karachi and parts of the USA, was a key player in the spy ring. During the last week of December 1993, he visited Trivandrum on a Sri Lankan passport and stayed in Hotel Fort Manor to strike a deal with me and Sasikumaran for secretly transferring the sensitive information pertaining to PSLV flights. Fauzia was also there at that time.

As per the deal, satellite launch data pertaining to atmospheric conditions (around 100 pages) available with the mainframe computer of ISRO and easily accessible to Sasikumaran; launch pad data (around 120 pages) available with Dr Morosov, a Russian in charge of "DB Salyut", a subsidiary of GK, or at Sriharikota (satellite launching station) and rocket testing facility data (140 pages) available with Dr Morosov or at Mahendragiri (satellite launching station) along with 12–13 pages of tridimensional drawings of launch pad machines were transferred to Pasha on different occasions.'

Chandrasekharan made some startling revelations that Mehboob Pasha had his eyes on many grey areas of India's defence and scientific establishments. He used Zuhaira to obtain such sensitive information.

'Thus, in March 1994, she contacted me and intimated that Pasha was interested in getting the topographical map of ADE, Bangalore, along with the details of aircraft assembly unit there, for which she offered US$15,000. I managed to procure these documents with the help of my friend S. K. Sharma who had well-placed contacts in that unit.

Pasha's another area of interest was the missile technology. During July 1994, Zuhaira approached me in Bangalore with a proposal to procure technology and personnel to undertake the project in Pakistan, for which Pasha was ready to make a remuneration of US$1 million and monthly payment of US$15,000 to each scientist/expert who would be engaged. I informed her that I would be in a position to meet the requirements as I was in good contact with three Russian scientists, namely Dr Kudredsev, Dr Lipitizihie and Dr Lapigin, who are experts in this field. Thus, during my visit to USSR in August 1994, I held discussions with Dr Kudredsev, who agreed to help me in this regard. However, I could not establish contacts with other two scientists and the proposal could not be worked out.'

While Nambi Narayanan's name was in the air for his alleged links with the espionage ring, he too prominently figured in Chandrasekharan's story along with certain details pertaining to ISRO's cryogenic engine project.

'ISRO and GK signed the agreement for the transfer of cryogenic technology during 1991. As per the agreement, GK was to provide technology and engines for a total consideration of around US$350–500 million. Initially, it was agreed that the Russian company should supply 12 engines. However, for almost two years, there was not much initiative from the Indian side. By the end of 1992, a new agency, namely Russian Space Agency (RSA), was formed with Yurikoptove, the deputy minister in charge of the project. The USA through their space agency (NASA) had signed agreements with RSA, by which certain restrictions were imposed over RSA in respect of the transfer of cryogenic technology from Russia to other countries. In view of these developments, GK had to modify certain terms and conditions of the agreement with ISRO after mutual discussions.'

In Chandrasekharan's disclosures, Nambi Narayanan was labelled as the kingpin of the spy network, with a conscious move to implicate him. Thus, he maintained:

'Nambi Narayanan, as senior ISRO scientist attached to cryogenic project, had frequent interaction with Russian scientists, notably Tcherkasov (mechanical engineer), Alexi Vasin (expert in electronics), Dr Kudredsev, Dr Lipitizihie and Dr Lapigin (experts in missile technology) and Sergi Savgarodvi (information department). Alexi helped him to transfer Vikas Engine technology to Brazil during 1989–1990. Vikas Engine is the re-model of Viking Engine which was initially developed by Arianespace Corporation (ASC) of France. Nambi Narayanan was attached to ASC during the period 1974–1979. Two companies—one from Ukraine and the other from Brazil—and the representative of GK in Brazil were involved in this transfer in which Nambi Narayanan and Alexi received payments. He was also instrumental for signing an agreement between ASC and a Mumbai-based firm, Hindustan Exports and Imports (HEI), in arranging satellite launching facilities for interested countries. For each launch, the ASC received US$1.5 billion of which the HEI got 3 per cent commission.'

Chandrasekharan in his story always tried to project the high level connections of the key players of espionage ring. Even the highest political executive was not spared in such attempts. On many instances, the overzealous interrogators had fallen in his trap and attached more credence to such disclosures. Thus, a Hyderabad-based firm, Machine Tools and Reconditions (MTAR) in which Prabhakar Rao, the son of former PM of India had business interests, was brought to the picture. He claimed that the aforementioned firm, at the instance of Nambi Narayanan, could manage to get a major contract with ISRO for the fabrication of the components of Vikas Engine. The public sector units like HAL who were also the bidders for the aforementioned contract were disqualified with a view to ensure the contract to MTAR group. In turn, MTAR helped Nambi Narayanan in transferring cryogenic engine technology/drawings of components, etc., to foreign countries and agencies on huge payments.

Chandrasekharan, with his unique personality, wide exposure within the country and abroad, corporate connections and network of contacts and friends in different fields, could easily weave a convincing espionage story with an exciting plot, different characters and crucial episodes. The concerned agencies, instead of making a thorough analysis of these disclosures, blindly forwarded them to the higher formations, as a result of which they could not retract from their claims and findings. Then they started the cover-up operations by using sections of media and other sources, which instead of resolving the complexities have further complicated the matter. Much blame should go against the investigators who too attached more credence to such revelations and blindly pursued a mirage that ultimately led them to serious troubles.

Equally pertinent were the glaring flaws in interrogation. Instead of an ideal interrogation team comprising of three members, personnel from different agencies gathered in the interrogation room and put forth relevant and irrelevant questions making the entire exercise a mockery. Though some of the interrogators tried to maintain the seriousness of the interrogation by upholding the basic principles of this tradecraft tool, soon everything went topsy-turvy due to the overenthusiastic and dubious approach by other interrogators. The interrogation during night was quite awesome. A couple of interrogators, bereft of any seriousness or commitment, comfortably slept in the room, while others were engaged in gossips and petty talks with the suspect, leaving the interrogation room an image of a railway retiring room with skeletal travellers!

There was no continuity in the interrogation. While one team left, the next team of interrogators stepped in without any proper briefing on the key revelations made by the suspect. Another serious lapse was the attempt by certain interrogators to put words into the mouth of the suspect based on their preconceived thinking or inputs from intelligence reports or office records or media gossips and cover stories. That has enabled the accused to come out with convincing statements in line with the desires of the interrogators!

THE GREAT SCIENTIST

8

When I arrived at the guest house, there was great excitement all around. Along the corridors and the steps leading to the first floor, I saw many new faces whose whispers and guarded talks created a grim situation.

I went directly to the first floor where the police investigators were busy in shifting Chandrasekharan to the jail. Kumar from the local Bureau headquarters was found in the midst of interrogators and investigators. The techies were busy in making new arrangements in the interrogation room. He came to me and said, 'SM's team has just arrested Nambi from his house. He will be brought here at any time. New teams have already arrived to interrogate him. But our local boss desires that you should be in the team.' Kumar went inside the interrogation room to oversee the arrangements.

I also accompanied him. The techies were engaged in heated discussions on how to improve the visual and audio clarity of the secret recordings of the interrogation. The local boss was not at all satisfied with the earlier recordings as images of certain interrogators were found along with the suspect. This, according to him, was a serious security lapse.

Near the main gate, we heard the long beeping sound of the police vehicles. Those at the corridors and the steps immediately disappeared. Accompanied by half a dozen police personnel in uniform and civvies, he was brought in.

He was a gentleman in golden grey trousers and glossy silk shirts. In his completely white hair and partially grey sporting beard, he looked older. His radiant face with sparkling eyes clearly reflected his intellectual acumen and strong will power and determination. Yet, in the midst of police personnel, he seemed totally embarrassed and confused.

The interrogation room was ready. The team members had already reached. Apart from Singh, who was the second-in-command of his boss supervising the operation, there were two new faces that appeared like typical wrestlers from the North. Maru from Delhi, who was associated with the questioning of other suspects, was conversing with the new interrogators.

Pot-bellied Nambi was seated in a wooden chair. The first team led by Singh started the initial questioning. Maru and I were the other two members, while a couple of personnel from other intelligence agencies and police were positioned at the corners. In his broken English typically in Hindi accent, he started putting stereotype questions.

'Do you know why you are brought here?' He relaxed in his revolving chair displaying total arrogance. His face exhibited such an expression that he was going to reveal something explosive that would explode the brain of the suspect!

'You know why you are brought here?' He shot another question with an idiotic smile.

Meanwhile, I observed the reaction of Nambi. He remained silent with an air of total contempt towards the interrogator.

'You should tell us why you are brought here?' His tone was full of anger and arrogance.

But that could not break his silence. This time, his stunning silence broke the interrogator's patience. He got up from his seat in a fit of anger to thrash Nambi.

'Hi, Singh Sahib, be patient; he will tell everything'. I intervened and controlled the situation. But I wondered why Singh had created such an awkward situation at the outset of the interrogation without properly understanding the suspect's mood and temper.

I felt that the hangover of many interrogators from using brute force against the suspects has decisive influence on their approach while dealing with suspects of all hues.

The sudden appearance of Singh's boss along with local sleuths surprised all of us. In his thick protruding moustache and pimpled face, the boss appeared as an arrogant officer full of ego and sadism. On seeing him, Singh was the first to jump up from his seat with folded hands. All the other interrogators followed the suit. An air of suspense filled the room. Nambi continued to sit on his chair without knowing the actual scene or the characters or their actual role. That had made him infuriated.

'Mr Singh, what bloody drama are you staging here? Is that how you people interrogate a fellow who betrayed the nation? See how relaxed and composed he is. Throw away his glossy shirt and trousers, let him remain naked. Then he will speak the truth!'

His words echoed in the room. There was sullen silence. I saw Singh virtually shivering with fear.

His bullying words did not create any impact over Nambi who continued to sit on the chair as if keenly waiting for some specific instructions.

'Hey, great scientist, I ask you to remove your clothes; or else I will ask my men to strip you fully naked.' His thunderous words reverberated in the room.

Nambi slowly stood up and started removing his clothes—shirt, vest and trousers. Left with underpants, he was almost fully naked.

'Yes, this is the way that we have to deal with traitors like him. You stand up in this posture and tell the truth to our interrogators.' He gleefully watched the scene as if he had done some great thing in his professional life. He had a few words with Singh who meekly accompanied his boss after entrusting the task of interrogation to his lieutenants.

The interrogation of Nambi continued. Semi-naked and humiliated, he stood like the statue of a devoted deity. I saw in his eyes an ocean of despair, frustration and agony which he tried to suppress and present a brave face before the interrogators: 'Now, may I ask you as why I am brought here?' With an element of authority, he posed the question to the interrogators.

'Mr Nambi, don't try to be over smart; you are no longer the great scientist of ISRO, but a wretched traitor booked by us. You come down from the glass house and cooperate with us or else your fate will be tragic.' The thick-moustached local sleuth who just joined the interrogation team gave a veiled threat.

Since the beginning of the operation, he was associated with the interrogation of Sasi along with interrogators from different agencies. In fact, he was acting on the behest of senior bosses with a preconceived mission of bursting a sensational espionage ring in Kerala!

'You people are calling me traitor time and again, but let me know what treason have I committed? Serving ISRO for many decades with full dedication and commitment?' Brave words of Nambi virtually stunned him. He fumbled for words to confront Nambi.

Then it was the turn of the compounder-turned interrogator, who like a wounded wrestler howled: 'You traitor, how dare you question our sir? You should not ask questions, but only speak truth.' Abruptly, his strong arm fell on the right cheek of Nambi. It was quite unexpected; darkness swept around him and he fainted on the ground. Panic-stricken interrogator left the team with our permission.

None of the interrogators anticipated such unruly behaviour from an interrogator. Later, I came to know that this fellow was inducted into the interrogation cell, at the instance of a senior boss who takes advantage of his services at the domestic front!

Nambi came back to senses after a couple of minutes. His right cheek was still swollen with pale bluish patches. I asked him to get seated. Shedding tears, he stared at me virtually with hundred questions on his face. His mind was full of anger, agony and frustration which he strongly desired to express through words. I felt certain that he is prepared to narrate his story.

'Born as the only son of a petty oil merchant in Nagercoil, Tamil Nadu, I was the only educated member of my family. My four sisters, not having much education, were married and settled in Trivandrum, Tirunelveli and Trichy. Some of them are still engaged in the making or selling of earthen pots for livelihood. I married Meena of Trivandrum in 1967. We have a son Sankarakumar and a daughter Geetha who is married to Arun, now working as an engineer in Vikram Sarabhai Space Centre (VSSC), Trivandrum. My son who completed M.Com is employed as computer operator in M/S Kurian E. Kalathil (KEK) Associates, Trivandrum. He also has an LPG dealership from SPIC Jyothi for Trivandrum north area.

I built my residential house in 8.5 cents plot at Perunthanni area Trivandrum in 1979–1980 for which I availed House Building Advance (HBA) of over ₹1 lakh from ISRO, besides funds from provident fund (PF), etc. I got a small plot of ancestral property in Tirunelveli, besides an inherited building of my wife at Kothuval Street Selam, which is given on rent.'

'Who is going to believe this story? We have specific information that you have huge deposits in half a dozen banks', the police officer from SM's crack team tried to demolish his claims.

'In one respect you are correct. Yes, I have accounts in five banks. But except the account in which my salary is credited, the outstanding balance in all other accounts is less than ₹1,000. I will give the details and you can check up on the same.'

I felt an element of honesty in his emphatic words.

'What about your salary and other perks from ISRO, apart from the commission and kickback from various deals and contracts?' I tried to unravel his professional life.

'I am working as deputy director in Liquid Propulsion Systems Centre (LPSC), Valiamala, Trivandrum in the grade of Scientist H with a basic pay of ₹7,300 per month. The total monthly salary inclusive of all allowances would be around ₹10,000. In fact, I had to go a long way to reach the scale.'

I felt that he strongly desired to unravel his professional story in ISRO. We patiently listened to his story.

'After graduating in mechanical engineering in 1965, I joined Thumba Equatorial Rocket Launching Station (TERLS) in September 1966 as technical assistant (design). On promotion as Scientist C in 1967, I joined Space Science and Technology Centre (SSTC) which was renamed as VSSC in 1973. In SSTC, I was mainly assigned with the task of developing Rohini Series Rockets using solid propulsion methods. Later, I concentrated in liquid propulsion system.'

'One major turning point in my career was the one-year programme in Princeton University, USA, for the advanced research in the field of solid propulsion under the guidance of Professor Martin Summerfield. Once fully convinced that liquid propulsion is the ideal technology for ISRO, I switched over to that field and worked under eminent scientists such as Luigi Crocco and David Harger that enabled me to obtain master's degree in space technology.

My knowledge and expertise in the field of propulsion had been enhanced through my two months' exposure in France during 1971 under ISRO–CNES collaboration programme. On return to India, I could successfully launch the first liquid propulsion rocket of 600 kg. Meanwhile, the efforts to launch a 3 ton liquid rocket met with a series of technical problems including the failure of a mission in 1973.

Thus, ISRO had explored other channels in pursuance of their mission of high thrust liquid rocket system. After a series of negotiations and discussions, a technical collaboration contract was signed between ISRO and Société Européenne de Propulsion (SEP),

France, in 1974 for the transfer of technology of Viking Engine. In fact, our aim was to acquire Viking Engine from France and indigenously develop it in ISRO.

The aforementioned agreement was unique as ISRO scientists could directly participate in the major operations and activities of SEP. Thus, a team of 40–50 engineers of ISRO who went to France to acquire the technology in 1977 was successful in obtaining know-how on fabrication assembly, testing and test result analysis. I headed the team that remained there till October 1979. I could discreetly collect large number of technical documents related to Viking Engine, cryogenic engine, test facilities and related fields from the French agency with the sole aim to take Indian space technology to new heights. Even some senior functionaries of ISRO like Professor Satish Dhawan who came to know about such operations during their visit to France advised me not to enter into such activities.'

'That means you started your spying operations years ago? The past experience might have helped you a lot in easily carrying out your present activities, isn't it?' I tried to corner him taking a clue out of his own story.

'Naturally, one might have such apprehensions. But my single point is that if I am presently involved in such activities, why I should disclose about my past operations of similar nature? What motivated me to do such adventurous and risky things in France was my desire to augment Indian space technology. Moreover, it was at my instance that ISRO was spearheading liquid propulsion system even relegating the solid propulsion methods in PSLV and allied fields.'

I felt that there was much logic in his arguments.

'A number of senior bureaucrats and scientists of ISRO were aware of my operations in Paris. Even Mr T. N. Seshan, the then space secretary, Government of India, was aware of such activities. All the documents and drawings procured from France were sent through the diplomatic bag of the Embassy of India in France.

Over 800 documents were transferred to India by using this channel. While the contractual documents were circulated to all concerned in VSSC, all other documents were kept under lock and key at the VSSC till the return of the entire ISRO team from France.'

'Ok Nambi, if such large number of senior bureaucrats and space scientists were well aware of your credentials and high integrity, why none of them has now come forward to defend you?' I confronted him with another query.

'Fine, naturally it is a genuine question. The truth is that you people have created a chimera of espionage and treason through orchestrated propaganda and campaign with help of media and other forces. In such a scenario, who will try to burn their fingers by openly defending a person with the label as "traitor"?'

I sincerely felt that there was some truth in his statement.

A section of media and some political masters in the state have already created a scenario that all the accused persons are traitors. Naturally, majority of the bureaucrats, keener to safeguard their career never dare to raise their small finger against any injustice or aberration from the part of the establishment, which they feel will adversely affect their future!

Nambi continued his story in despair and agony.

'On my return to India, our team systematically made use of these documents for the development of Vikas Engine which was later renamed as Viking Engine. However, all was not well with my professional side; unfortunately, I became a victim of the ego and professional rivalries of my senior bosses. That was in 1982 when the then director of VSSC was at loggerheads with my immediate boss and had some misunderstanding that I helped him out of the way at hierarchical level. That ultimately led to an in-house vigilance probe against me.'

He stopped for a moment and watched our response.

'Oh Nambi, you are really smart; you want to pre-empt something specific against your so-called integrity and reputation. Isn't it?'

I tried to give an impression that we know all about the story that he tried to unfold.

'I fear that the hangover of that incident still haunts me; that is why I like to spell out the real truth; you people may believe it or not—that is a different story.' He was blunt in his reply and continued.

'The director was waiting for an opportunity to fix me under one pretext or other and dislodge me from my assignment. During that period, the then commandant of the Central Industrial Security Force (CISF) attached to our unit joined hands with the director and framed false charges against me. The stores officer who was close to the commandant made a complaint to the latter that I had received ₹25,000 as bribe from the suppliers of office furniture. Instead of ascertaining the real facts or collecting evidence, the director transferred me from the active post of the project director of PS-2 of VSSC on the basis of a report submitted by the commandant. It was at this point I came to know about the false charges fabricated against me. I approached the chairman for a full-fledged enquiry, based on which I was reinstated in my original assignment. This decision has irked the director. The commandant was immediately shifted from the CISF unit at VSSC.'

'Mr Nambi, you have successfully defended your case, but there are many missing links which make it less credible and convincing. Basically, it is difficult to believe that an in-house vigilance probe is concluded and action taken without knowledge of the charged officer. There are some basic procedures that should be complied in any in-house probe or departmental proceedings; the charged officer has the privilege or right to defend his case.'

I clarified our stand with a veiled warning that we cannot be taken for a ride with such cock and bull stories.

Thus, he again switched over to his professional life in ISRO.

'We could make further advancement in developing Viking Engine technology. ISRO could produce its prototype in 1983–1984, which was hot-wired in 1985 from France. In this regard, I visited France twice in 1985 to test the Engine and related tasks.

ISRO's next priority was to make engines for high altitude flight testing. A Swedish firm, M/S Volvo, was engaged to supply three engines, whereas special systems and tankages, etc., were procured from other countries like France. By the end of 1991, India could develop the engines and stage systems. Thus, during the first successful launch of PSLV-D2 in 1994, a combination of liquid and solid propulsion systems were used in different stage systems.

My interests were more in the area of liquid propulsion. Since the formation of LPSC in 1987, I remained attached to the unit except for a brief period of 14–15 months in Bangalore. Along with liquid propulsion system, I was also actively associated with task of developing cryogenic engines.

In cryogenic engines, liquid propulsion system is used with liquid hydrogen and liquid oxygen at very low temperature. Only a few countries such as the USA, erstwhile USSR, France, China and Japan have this technology. India is striving hard to develop this technology for its Geosynchronous Satellite Launch Vehicle (GSLV) programme.

It is in this connection that the GK came into the picture. ISRO has entered into an agreement with this Russian firm for providing technology transfer and supply of three numbers of cryogenic engines and its stages. But in 1992–1993, Russians breached the contract under American pressure, saying that they have restrictions on the transfer of technology; instead, they would supply seven engines and stages instead of three engines earlier agreed upon. But before the breach of contract, ISRO had received some drawings of cryogenic engines, components and stages. The big question before the ISRO scientists was whether they could indigenously develop cryogenic engine with such incomplete drawings.'

'Thus, you thought of making quick money by selling out these incomplete drawings to interested parties especially after your decision to take voluntary retirement from ISRO?' Maru posed a logical question.

'Sir, that was totally untrue. I have never thought of doing such things in my life. There were compelling reasons for my decision to apply for voluntary retirement.' For a while, I saw a different Nambi totally depressed and frustrated with a reddening face. Then he started to unravel many things from his personal life.

'In fact, since the early 1993, I was feeling dejected with my work due to domestic and official reasons. When my wife led a highly religious and spiritual life, I felt more isolated and depressed at home especially after spending long hours in office. In order to get relief from boredom, I explored other vocations.'

'Did you come across these Maldivian ladies during this period?' Officer from SM's crack team tried to establish his links with Mariam and Fauzia.

'I have never met these ladies in my life. I don't know who fabricated this story. I have nothing to hide; if so why should I reveal my past episodes and incidents?' I felt some element of sincerity and uprightness in his words.

'Ok, then why haven't you left ISRO? Is there any hidden agenda for you to continue?' I tried to avert his move to take us on a ride focusing his personal life.

'I was serious in my decision to quit ISRO; in August 1994, I discussed the matter with the chairman who agreed to relieve me after the successful launch of PSLV-2. Despite my decision to leave, I sincerely worked for the success of the project,' he stopped for a moment as if trying to recollect something from the past.

'Obviously, your story fits into the disclosures made by Chandrasekharan and Sasikumaran, but with some major contradictions.' It was the turn of Maru to derail his claims.

'I don't know what disclosures they have made. Everyone has their own stories, which may be true or untrue. I have my own impressions about them.' He remained unmoved of interrogator's attempt to embarrass him.

'Definitely you know a lot about them, as you were their close partners in the entire deal?' I posed the question to bring out the nature of his relations with Sasi and Chandrasekharan.

Nambi didn't show any reservations to disclose all what he knew about Sasikumaran and Chandrasekharan.

'In the 1970s–1980s, Sasikumaran was attached to VSSC and working at Satellite Launch Vehicle (SLV)-3. Following some scandal, he was transferred to LPSC during 1990–1991. In LPSC, as deputy general manager, he was in charge of the fabrication of PS-3 Engine and was directly reporting to another senior officer. He was never part of the team evolving in Vikas Engine, but was associated with the indigenization of thrust chamber material with a Hyderabad-based team. What I wanted to clarify is that Sasikumaran has never been my subordinate officer.'

'But, in many respects, you were birds of the same feather and flocked together in many scandals and illegalities, isn't it?' The interrogator from SM's crack team was trying to establish that they were partners in the present case as well.

'Sorry Sir, that is not correct. I have visited his house once or twice till date. Besides we have attended common dinner with Russian delegation and ISRO officials on three or four times. But in such get-togethers we never discussed any official matters or the shady deals. As far as I know, Sasikumaran has no personal or professional rivalry with me.

But the case of Chandrasekharan is different. I met him for the first time in 1991 when our delegation was on the way to Russia. The inebriated Chandrasekharan who introduced himself as the agent of GK, Russia, created an ugly scene in the flight. Thus, on landing at the airport, I checked up his details with Professor Duyenv, the chairman of GK, who confided to me that Chandrasekharan was not their liaison agent for ISRO matters.'

'Then, how he claimed and operated as representative of GK and interacted with all key officials of ISRO?' Maru tried to clarify.

'In fact, for more than one decade, he has been exploring all means to become the agent of GK in India. Even when our delegation was in Russia, he personally requested me to recommend his case to Professor Duyenv, which I flatly refused as the policy of ISRO was not to engage intermediate agents. While I was on an official visit to Bangalore in 1991, he invited me for a dinner in which he again made this request. This time also I didn't plead his case. Later, I came to know that he managed to become the representative of GK, with the help of Alexi, who was known to Chandrasekharan for more than one decade.'

'Who was this Alexi? How he developed close intimacy with Chandrasekharan?' Consciously I tried to get more inputs about this Russian who figured prominently in the statements of Chandrasekharan and others.

I saw a mischievous smile on Nambi's face, but he continued.

'Alexi operated as the key functionary of GK in India, but many of us in ISRO suspected him as a Russian secret agent. I met him for the first time when the Russian delegation visited India in 1990 for finalizing the details of cryogenic engine contract. He used to accompany the delegates even during conference sessions. But he never participated in the discussions. From his behaviour, I gathered an impression that he was a secret agent deputed to closely monitor the activities of Russian delegates.'

'Have you brought your apprehensions about Alexi to the notice of ISRO authorities?' Maru was quick to corner him from his own words.

'I didn't, as I had no concrete inputs to substantiate my doubts. Moreover, it was a crucial phase of cryo engine discussions. However, ISRO officials were very cautious in dealing with Alexi. In one of our visits to Moscow, he explored the possibility of ISRO purchasing milling engine from Ukraine and not from Russia. He arranged a meeting with representatives of a Ukrainian firm. From the discussions, we got a strong feeling that there was something fishy in the deal, and hence we didn't move ahead with proposal. Subsequently, we came to know that there were some underhand moves to siphon off huge commissions from that firm.'

'Do you think that Chandrasekharan, as a close ally of Alexi, was also interested in such deals to pocket share of such commissions?' I tried to verify certain claims made by Chandrasekharan through Nambi.

'Yes, I had no doubt that he was hand in glove with Alexi in such deals. His frustration on not materializing certain interested contracts has also led to his personal grudge against me. He felt that I deprived him of getting commission from Russians on account of the launch of INSAT-2C and INSAT-2D. We had started the launching of INSAT series satellite during 1988–1990 for which global tenders were floated. The USA, Russia and the French were the main bidders. The first series of tenders were awarded to the French company ASC. When the second round of global tenders was floated in 1993, the Russians were keen to win the tender for which Chandrasekharan was quite active. However, this time also order went to the same French company. Though I was not a member of the committee that finalized tender, rumours were in the air that I pulled the strings in favour of the French company. No doubt, it was a matter of great heartburn to him as the award was worth ₹100 to ₹150 crore for each launch. You can well imagine the commission lost by Chandrasekharan!'

Reading between the lines of the revelations made by Nambi and Chandrasekharan, I felt certain that the latter, in many respects, was inimical to the former. Thus, during sustained interrogation, Chandrasekharan found an easy escape route to save himself from the pressure of the interrogators to present Nambi as the kingpin of all shady deals. While winding up day's interrogation and returning to the office, I was in doubt whether our findings would be endorsed by the senior bosses or not?

Back to the office, I found hectic activity everywhere. The nodal officer and team were busy in drafting the next team of interrogators. Every Tom, Dick and Harry of the local headquarters were in his room along with half a dozen new faces from outstation units.

I saw a tense and impatient nodal officer in their midst.

'Where were you all this time? We are yet to send a detailed statement on the disclosures of Nambi; the headquarters has reminded us a couple of times. Our local boss is quite upset. You scribble the important points; we have to meet the boss immediately and to brief him before drafting the report.'

He was like a fish out of water.

I felt exasperated of his words. After all, systematic interrogation is not a child's play. I failed to understand as why all this hurry; the sky is not going to fall down if there is some delay in sending the report. And what should we send to the headquarters—all cock and bull stories narrated by the suspects? Truths, half-truths or full of lies! But I kept my nerves cool.

'Sir, I have already jotted down the points, if the senior boss is free, we can meet him and discuss the points.'

The boss was alone in his room, struggling with an important draft that appeared like the messy manuscript of a new author. He signalled us to take our seats, but continued the pitched battle in the draft with zigzagged red and green lines and writings that can be deciphered only by an amateur astrologer!

'I am fed up with your fellows who send all these notes without any head and tail, making no sense. Ask them to ensure more clarity and brevity in their drafts; that will save much of my time.' A visibly annoyed boss bundled a bunch of files and turned to us.

'I learnt that fellow Nambi was broken and started telling the truth. Not only our headquarters but the state police chief and others are much interested on his disclosures.' He paused for a moment to get our feedback.

A thoroughly shaken nodal officer had nothing to comment; he glumly looked at me, as if I had something sensational to share with the boss.

'Sir, he has started talking to us, but all about his personal and professional life and activities, and achievements in ISRO. It appears that he is not so affluent or well off as projected in the media; even some of his sisters eke out a living by selling potteries in the open market.'

I told him candidly.

'Who is interested in such personal or professional stories? Our concern is as how he operated in the espionage gang betraying the vital secrets of space technology?' I sensed a harsher tone in his words.

'He hasn't spelt anything specific in this direction; on the contrary, his claim was that all through his life he sincerely worked for the advancement of the country's space technology even risking his career while remaining in France', I tried to explain my impressions on Nambi.

'Some of our field reports also indicated that all his close relations are struggling to meet their both ends. And this fellow Nambi is also not lavish in his life style. His son is yet to find a decent job.'

Surprisingly, the nodal officer opened his mouth and anxiously waited for the response of the local boss.

'That means he has taken you people for a smooth ride. We know a lot about his nefarious activities. Do you think that we the Bureau people were sleeping here without cataloguing the dubious activities of scientists like Nambi.' I felt certain that the boss has preconceived notions or misconceptions about this scientist.

'Sir, he has come out with all such personal weakness—drinking habits, etc., but never spelt a single word about his shady deals with foreign agents.' The nodal officer became totally silent, but I tried to make my stand clear.

'That is the point that you should take note of: a man—whether a scientist or a soldier or bureaucrat—bereft of moral strength and character can stoop to any level and easily fall in the trap of women, who maybe disguised as trained agents. This has what exactly happened in the case of these scientists. We want to hear it from their own mouth; that is your task.'

The boss cut short the meeting.

Out of boss' room, the nodal officer was in a lighter vein.

'Now your task is clear, isn't it? Let him speak the truth as how he betrayed the nation and sold the vital secrets of ISRO. Today or tomorrow, he will spill the beans. I am sure that our new team will concentrate on this task.'

I wondered as how he was so confident.

While returning to the hotel, the words of senior boss echoed in my ears: 'cataloguing the dubious activities of the scientists, etc.', authoritative and confident words of a senior sleuth! But he never pondered over a moment as how such inputs were collected? Who collected such information? How reliable such inputs are?

The cruel reality was that majority of such inputs were regularly generated by field staff for their survival. Sometimes, compelled by circumstances, they make mountains out of molehills and script out stories with their own imagination. By blindly incorporating such stories—truth or untruth—in the professional horoscope of great scientists, perhaps, you are preparing the hangman's noose for them, especially when they come under cloud for so-called offences under Official Secrets Act!

COLOURFUL NARRATION OF A SENIOR SCIENTIST

9

Back in the hotel, I was in a whirlpool of distressed thoughts when different images of Nambi appeared alive. Many poignant questions stirred up my subconscious: If he is innocent, how callous and cruel we are in ruining his career, reputation and family! Who can compensate for such loss inflicted over him?

However, those whispering voices were shushed by the practical side of my mind configured by years of training and working in the organization: 'such mundane thoughts have no place in your profession; you confront suspects—some are genuine, some fake and some others totally innocent!'

I came closer to the window; across the road, I saw the graffiti glittering in red light 'Lal Restaurant cum Bar'; the same place that Nambi used to visit to unbundle his distressed emotions.

The restaurant was almost empty, but the hustle and bustle of the bar made the place lively. I went inside the bar and occupied an empty table at the corner. While sipping the red liquid, what figured in my mind was his image—the renowned scientist who spent in solitude on many late evenings at the corner of this bar! I was simulating the same situation and experience by putting myself in his shoes.

I returned to the room and waited for the arrival of my colleague sharing the room. He has been tirelessly working to establish a typical espionage case on the whims and fancies of his masters! For the last couple of days, he was associated with the interrogation of a key suspect. One of his co-interrogator was a unique expert in making a mountain out of a molehill!

Soon, he stepped in: a medium built, dark-complexioned person in his late 40s. I saw a rare sparkle on his face, which normally had a melancholic look.

'Richard, did you have your dinner?' Sitting criss-cross on the bed, he asked. Without waiting for my response, he continued: 'We had our dinner with our Delhi people, who brought some hot stuff too. Really, it was a day for us to celebrate; the great scientist we had taken from Ahmedabad has started to spill the beans.' I found him in high spirits.

'You know, we people work day and night, sometimes with empty stomach, but these fellows who live in glass houses eat, drink and merry, and even sell the nation to lead their luxurious life. You would be stunned if you hear their real-life story.'

Now I am convinced that the hot stuff has started affecting his cerebral senses.

My studied silence energized him to narrate the story.

'This ISRO scientist Dr Sasi, originally from Quilon district, married to a doctor and having a daughter and a son—both married and well settled, passed mechanical engineering from the prestigious College of Engineering, Trivandrum, as early as in 1962. After a brief stint in Hindustan Steels Ltd, he joined ISRO in late 1970, had associated with its various operations such as Rocket Fabrication Facility (RFF), SLV, industrial liaison and planning, LPSC and cryo engine fabrication, before joining Space Application Centre (SAC) in Ahmedabad in 1994. He had two deputation assignments to Moscow (Russia) during 1992–1993.

He, for the first time, met Chandrasekharan of GK in 1991, when a Russian delegation was on a visit to Trivandrum. The meeting was arranged through a common friend who worked in Kerala Hitech, Trivandrum. Later, in mid-1991, as a member of the Indian delegation consisting ISRO scientists and industrial representatives, he visited Russia for around 20 days. Chandrasekharan was also with them as liaison man.

In subsequent visits to Russia, Chandrasekharan, representing GK, introduced Russian counterparts to senior ISRO scientists including Sasi. In turn, he frequently visited ISRO establishments in Trivandrum and Bangalore, and interacted with scientists and other senior personnel. Chandrasekharan could easily pick up the weakness of some of these top officers, mainly exploiting three W's (wine, women and wealth) commonly used in espionage.

You know, he himself has revealed his sexual escapades. He picked up German and French languages not for mere interaction with scientists and technical experts in those countries, but to make a way into the hearts of beautiful ladies!'

I felt that my colleague was eager to narrate such stories of sexual escapades that had filled my mind with the flashy images of Bill Clinton and Monica Lewinsky in the royal secluded chambers of White House!

'Perhaps the intelligent scientist might have rightly sensed your real interests and have taken the interrogators for a ride by narrating those fancied stories. Actually, you have fallen in his trap?' My blunt response made him a little irritated, but he continued his story.

'Do you think that we have swallowed whatever he vomited; our team members were not such fools. We extracted truth through questioning and cross-questioning and picking up contradictions from his statements. Sometimes, our people lost temper and handled him nicely! There were a few interesting anecdotes too.'

My colleague went into loud laughter, which he could not control for a few seconds.

I wondered what would be this interesting episode in a serious interrogation of a reputed space scientist suspected in a sensational espionage case! However, I kept my nerves cool and waited to hear the story.

'Our Singhji misunderstood "Fiji" as a common colloquial slang in his area connected to sex. The scientist has to bear the brunt for his poor power of understanding and his inability to follow the English accent. We had a tough time to convince him that "Fiji" is one of the satellite launching stations frequently used by ISRO for launching their satellites.'

My colleague couldn't stop his laughter, but what came to my mind were the poignant words of Nambi: 'If these people who cannot differentiate between a rocket and missile run the great IPS, and intelligence and security organizations, what would be ultimate fate of this great nation and millions of people?'

'Then, why the officers like Singhjis are deputed for the interrogation of senior scientists of ISRO?' My words evoked scornful response from him.

'Your problem is that you have never worked in other places; there are dozens of Singhjis attached to many senior bosses. They would well look after their domestic chores such as accompanying their better halves to beauty salons, taking kids to schools and doing all marketing for home and what not! In return, they would be compensated by such assignments or frequent tours and rewards.'

He lighted a cigarette and continued the story.

'Nambi, who was heading the cryo systems project at LPSC, brought Sasi into the espionage network during 1989–1990. Nambi had some secret deals with a private firm in France. In April 1990, he mooted the idea to sell the technology of Vikas Engine to Pakistan, for which he sought the assistance of Alexi Vasin of GK. Their secret mission was to transfer the complete drawings of Vikas Engine, the photocopies of which were arranged by Sasi.

These drawings—some 50–60 bundles/rolls—were passed to that IG of police, who arranged the transfer of these documents to Moscow through Ural Aviation. Alexi, on receipt of these consignments in Moscow, was assigned to dispatch them to St Petersburg from where it was taken by road to Amsterdam. From Amsterdam, these parcels were taken to Pakistan by air. The payments for the consignments were made by Pakistan to Alexi who in turn paid the remuneration to Nambi, Sasi and others. They received the first payment of ₹10 lakh. Alexi also arranged two weeks free trip for Nambi and Sasi in Switzerland and West Germany in 1991.'

As the disclosures of Nambi were still afresh in mind, I felt aghast as how the interrogators of Sasi are building up an espionage story from nothing.

'How far these bundles of drawings would help the actual technology transfer especially in the case of Vikas Engine? Whether a senior police officer of the rank of IG would directly involve in such deals?' My query annoyed my friend, but he tried to convince me of the marvellous work that they had done to collect such inputs!

'You don't know anything about corporate or technology espionage. The corporate houses or scientific establishments work for years and spend huge amounts to develop new patents or technology like Vikas Engine. A number of scientists or technical experts spend the prime of their life working on such projects. Officially, what they gain out of their success in such projects is compliments or accolades from their higher-ups or political masters. On the contrary, if they sell out or transfer the developed patents or technologies to interested parties through espionage, they would be really hitting the jackpot that they can never imagine in their entire life.'

He posed himself as an expert in unravelling the mysterious areas of espionage and continued.

'Alexi is the kingpin of these operations; he is now exploring the possibility of selling Vikas Engine technology to other countries.

Besides, Pakistan, Indonesia, Taiwan and Brazil are keen to procure this technology. A consignment of drawings already sent to Alexi is now lying at Moscow air cargo, for which a deal has been struck with North Korea on a consideration of ₹60–70 lakh. Another five sets of drawings, each weighing around 40 kg, are now kept preserved at different safe houses in Trivandrum area at the instance of Nambi, Sasi and their accomplices. One of these sets is meant for Pakistan on a payment of ₹45 lakh.'

While he was unfolding this espionage story with characters, places and episodes trotting across the globe, I felt like witnessing the Hollywood spy thriller *From Russia with Love*. Its celluloid characters—MI6 super-agent James Bond; Red Grant, the dreaded assassin; M, chief of British Intelligence; and Ali Kerim Bey, their head in Istanbul; Tatiana, the beautiful Soviet cipher clerk sent to entice Bond; Rosa Klebb, the dashing girl operative of Russian Intelligence; Sylvia Trench, the sexy girlfriend of Bond and others (men and women playing the cloak and dagger operations with sex, blackmail and killings to procure a lector cryptographic device from the Soviets)—flashed through my mind.

I was astonished as what happened to such beautiful and dangerous dames of our espionage story. My colleague could easily decipher my anxiety and continued the narration.

'You see, three Maldivian women—Zuhaira, operating from Colombo; Fauzia based in Bangalore and Mariam Rasheeda shuttling between Malé and Trivandrum—were the key players of the operation.'

'Nambi introduced Zuhaira to Sasi at Hotel Fort Manor, Trivandrum, during March–June 1990 when a Russian delegation was staying there. Zuhaira was also introduced to Alexi. Since then, she was a frequent visitor to Trivandrum, Bangalore and Chennai as part of her clandestine mission of collecting secret documents from those scientists and making payments. She used Sri Lankan, Indian and Maldivian passports for her frequent trips to India. She was a smart lady with some scientific knowledge.'

During another meeting with her at Hotel Pankaj, Trivandrum, in April 1991, she evinced interest in cryo and Viking technologies to meet the requirements of her Pak handlers. Thus, the first set of Viking Engine drawings managed by Nambi from LPSC was delivered to her. She personally carried the same to Delhi en route to the final destination in Pakistan. Subsequent meetings between Zuhaira and Nambi were held in Bangalore during June 1992 and May 1993 when secret deals were struck for the delivery of PSLV data/drawings in which Pakistan was interested. She played a crucial role in the negotiations between these scientists and a key figure of the Pakistan Atomic Energy Commission.'

My colleague was minutely narrating the daredevil operations of Zuhaira, almost on the lines of Mata Hari, the legendary spy who worked for Germany during the First World War by seducing senior defence officers of allied forces! So ridiculous was his story on Zuhaira that I felt like laughing, but I controlled myself with some genuine doubts.

'I wonder as what magic this lady plays to seduce these senior scientists and police officers for a dangerous game? Surprisingly, even the scientists of Atomic Energy Commission dance to her tunes? How can we believe these disclosures?' I was quite sure that the entire thing was a concocted story well-articulated by a suspect under duress. I have other doubts too.

But my colleague, brushing aside such doubts, continued.

'You will be surprised if you hear about their operations targeting our space and defence establishments. As part of the transfer of PSLV drawings and technology, a number of secret meetings between Zuhaira and these two scientists were held at various places including Bangalore and Trivandrum during 1993–1994. Finally, a deal was struck by fixing the remuneration as US$0.9 million.

For the transfer of drawings/documents, a secret meeting was held at Hotel Luciya in Trivandrum on 23–24 September 1994. Prior to the meeting, Mohammed Aslam, the scientist from Pakistan along with his associate Abdul Haleel and three others occupied rooms in the hotel. Zuhaira was staying in Room No. 108. The meeting took place in that room, whereas the two scientists, the IG and Chandrasekharan met together and the transfer of documents and payments were made in the presence of Zuhaira and Aslam. Bundles of US dollars (0.9 million) were kept by Nambi.'

Another scene of *From Russia with Love* flashed through my mind, when he stopped for a moment to light another cigarette. But what really surprised me were the key characters of his narrative.

'Are Aslam and Haleel the same names going around in the files of various secret organizations since long for their alleged attempts to penetrate our nuclear and atomic establishments? I wonder how such a prominent scientist of the hostile country easily step into our area and meet senior space scientists.'

I was quite sure that some interrogators—knowingly or unknowingly—might have put these names in his mouth to verify such reports!

'No doubt, many of his disclosures have authenticated our reports on the efforts of Pakistan to penetrate the sensitive establishments in our area. Perhaps, we failed to unearth their network or sleeping cells. After all, they use all ingenious tradecraft mechanisms to continue their clandestine activities. Who knows that Aslam and others might have landed in our place in assumed identity, using fake passports or documents?'

I felt that my colleague has convincing explanations to ensure credibility to his filmy story!

Then he narrated the story of Fauzia who, according to him, was a born spy, well versed with all tradecraft mechanisms in espionage.

'It was Chandrasekharan who first introduced Fauzia to Sasi at Indiranagar Club, Bangalore. After a gap of around one month, he again met her at the same Club when initial discussions were made on the cryo engine technology. Another meeting between the two was held at Hotel Devas, Trivandrum, during October 1991, followed by the next meeting at Indiranagar Club, Bangalore, in November 1991 when Chandrasekharan was also present. During these meetings, discussions on the transfer of Vikas Engine drawings/technology were made.

In 1992, they had three other similar meetings in Bangalore during April, August and December, when the details of the transfer of drawings and technology of Vikas Engine were discussed and finalized. In April meeting, held at Indira Club, she handed over ₹1.5 lakh to Sasi as initial payment, while she paid ₹5,000 to him during the August meeting as advance payment for the delivery of Vikas Engine drawings.'

I felt this part of the story was almost on the lines of the confession statement of Fauzia, videographed by a team of interrogators with much fanfare. Thus, the intentions of some of the interrogators were clear to me, but I kept my silence and keenly listened to his narration.

'Again, it was Chandrasekharan, who introduced Mariam to Sasi after her visit to Bangalore during September 1994. On Chandra's tip-off, he visited Hotel Samrat, Trivandrum, where she was put up along with Fauzia. During his second meeting, he took her for dinner to a star hotel in Trivandrum and developed close intimacy with her. He was so particular to take her alone without antagonizing her roommate Fauzia who was keen to visit ISRO establishments in and around Trivandrum. Thus, on a holiday, he arranged a taxi and took Fauzia to LPSC Valiamala and spent some time at his office there.'

The nicely woven espionage story evoked two crucial questions in my mind: Whether the suspected scientist is blessed with such imagination to incorporate all such nuggets of the art of spying? Or his so-called revelations were nothing but the creation of interrogators? Meanwhile, my colleague continued his narration.

'You see, the key players of spy ring had a crucial meeting at Madras International Hotel on 24 January 1994 to explore the possibility of the supply of Russian tanks to interested countries. This idea has originated in Sasi's mind after his visit to Salda in Russia where tanks with high manoeuvrability were manufactured. He gathered inputs that these tanks which have good demand in many countries like Malaysia were available at a cost of ₹45 lakh each, as against the international market price of ₹2.5 crore. The meeting entrusted Zuhaira, her friend Robertson and Fauzia to find out the potential buyers. Other projects such as the setting up of a factory for the manufacture of bulletproof vests by using carbon cloth technology have also come up for discussion. This consortium has also plans to purchase an offshore fishing vessel from Jetlines for a cost of ₹14 crore of which ₹4 crore have already been paid as advance. The vessel was expected to be delivered during February 1995.

The capital needed for these ventures/projects would be mobilized from the pooled money deposited by them in two accounts operated by Nambi in Bangalore branch of the Bank of Rajasthan. Parekh, the chairman of the Bank, stationed at Jodhpur, is hand in glove with Nambi and others in maintaining an escrow account in which the money generated through fraudulent/illegal deals are deposited/transacted. The dollar and other foreign currencies received by them are also exchanged by the bank with total immunity.'

He finished with a satisfactory smile.

It was getting late; the lengthy narration of the story exhausted my colleague, but he felt elated by their wonderful achievement of extracting leading clues from the suspect.

*

The canards and falsehoods cannot be buried under the carpet for long. After a couple of weeks in a chance meeting with Hari, the CBI officer with whom I had personal friendship for decades, the cat was out of the bag, I was surprised on hearing his words of accolades: 'You sleuths had done a wonderful job in busting an international espionage racket! I was thrilled on going through the revelations made by one of the space scientists during the interrogation; how meticulously you have built up a concrete espionage case!' He continued in his sarcastic style: 'I had the burden of again questioning the scientist Sasikumaran as part of our investigation. What we could gather from him was that he had taken your interrogators for a ride by narrating a convincing espionage story based on his vast exposure and experience.'

Hari's words didn't surprise me; even a layman can reach such surmises by reading between the lines of the disclosures religiously followed by the interrogators. But I kept my impressions guarded to ascertain his findings.

'That means, he is not in any way connected with the case', I raised my genuine doubts.

'The real fact is that he could easily read the intentions of the interrogators. Thus, he made revelations that were far from truth; mere figments of imagination that were nicely cobbled together to escape from the pressure of the interrogators, who were keen to establish an espionage case! But we investigators go after concrete evidence.'

He started talking like a professional investigator listing out the details of such distortions and fallacies.

'It is true that the scientist along with his doctor wife met Mariam on a tip-off by Chandrasekharan. But this meeting was not for any espionage, but to explore the scope of starting a multi-storeyed lodge in Trivandrum for the visiting Maldivians, by converting his rented building in the city. Similarly, Fauzia contacted him seeking his help in connection with her daughter's new visa and her admission in a Bangalore school.'

Hari was emphatic that no suspicious relations with these Maldivian ladies could be unearthed.

'Do you think that this gentleman has done everything for these ladies out of his philanthropic zeal or for something else?' I had my own doubts.

'Truly speaking, we haven't peeped into the personal life of the suspect. We looked for specific evidences to establish an act of espionage or the violation of the provisions under Official Secrets Act. Generally, we are guided by some misconception that those persons known for their faintness for three W's (wine, women and wealth) are susceptible to espionage. If that be the case, the whole world would be flooded with master spies and agents who would lay their hands on everything safe and secure.'

I felt that there was much logic on his argument: all people with ostensible weaknesses need not be traitors and all those preaching patriotism need not be true saints!

But the story built around another Maldivian lady, namely Zuhaira, was horrendous. Sasi has never come across such a lady, nor Nambi or others. The only logic was that this Mata Hari-like character was born in the brain of somebody with the sinister motive to script a fancied espionage story. Once she ceased to exist as the key character of this espionage network, the whole story crumbled like a pack of cards.

Same was the case with other players such as the IG of police, Mohammed Aslam, Abdul Haleel, Robertson and others—a whole lot of agents and subagents created by the interrogators or investigators. The so-called crucial meeting attended by the key players of the network at Madras International Hotel on 24 January 1994 was yet another episode consciously scripted by them to suit their storyline! Hari was really pointing accusing fingers against those interrogators and investigators for those major professional lapses.

I patiently listened to his observations and findings.

'But the most crucial aspect was that Sasi based on certain real facts and episodes could weave a convincing espionage story before the interrogators who swallowed it as such giving new dimensions to the case. The significant strides in space technology, his official and personal trips to a number of foreign countries and above all close contacts with ISRO scientists and others like

Nambi, Chandrasekharan, Alexi and so on, enabled him to add more flesh and blood to this story, much to the satisfaction of his interrogators! Thus, he created sensational images of Ural Aviation flights with tonnes of sensitive drawings/documents on Vikas Engine/PSLV that had been airlifted from different stations in India moving to Moscow, St Petersburg en route to Amsterdam and finally to Islamabad.'

'What about his disclosures pertaining to their moves to start the supply/trade of Russian tanks and other ventures?' He burst into laughter on hearing my query.

'Perhaps this was the funniest story, as the real things were entirely different. Actually, Sasi, during his visit to Russia in 1994, had interaction with Dr Alexander Brooke and Ustinov of MDB Aviation, Moscow, which was in the process of signing an agreement with Bangalore-based HAL for the manufacture of 300 aircrafts with a capacity of 200 passengers each in India. The initial working capital for the project was to the tune of US$500 million. Chandrasekharan through his Cochin-based businessman tried to raise this capital as loan from certain banks/financiers in Kuwait. When this move failed to take off, the project was abandoned.

Dr Brooke who had long years of experience in aviation industry in USSR, particularly those related to MIG aircrafts and engines, launched another venture of manufacturing power plants of 20 MW capacity using these old engines. Though he tipped of Sasi as the principal consultant of his Indian project, he did not accept it as he was still in ISRO undertaking sensitive assignments connected with cryogenic technology. Meanwhile, Sasi, in view of his close contacts with Dr Brooke, made a suggestion to MDB Aviation to get in touch with senior ISRO officials for entering into a contract with ISRO in airlifting certain ISRO materials from Russia.'

Hari was emphatic that nothing incriminating or any specific evidence linking the scientist's connections with any foreign agencies or agents could be unearthed. The unresolved question before him was as why the interrogators and investigators scripted an espionage story out of nothing? Whether it was due to lack of professionalism or at the instance of some extraneous forces? Such doubts haunted me too when Hari left the annexe of the government guest house situated in the heart of the city!

THE FORCED CONFESSION   10

My colleague, after his splendid narration of the disclosures of the accused scientist, had fallen into a deep slumber, but in the adjacent bed of the double room suite, sleep had evaded me for long. Whenever I closed my eyes, the images of the various new characters of the story flashed through my mind. In the inner canvass of my mind, I drew a blueprint of how Nambi should be confronted with these details during the next stage of interrogation.

The next morning when we reached the interrogation centre to replace the team that had interrogated Nambi during the previous night, they were in a hurry to leave the place without giving us a feedback on the inputs gathered by them. I felt it was rather a coincidence that the night team was headed by the same officer who managed to get the confession of Fauzia that was videographed.

As news was already in air that the CBI would take over the investigation of the case at any time, the Special Investigation Team (SIT) had shown a lukewarm approach in his interrogation. Same was the case with other agencies except a few senior officers who were bent upon unearthing espionage network. Thus, our team was present for interrogation along with a police officer.

When we stepped into the interrogation room, we saw a thoroughly shattered and shaken Nambi. In his stooping posture, we saw in his eyes an ocean of despair, frustration and helplessness. On seeing us, he slowly turned his eyes away from us, as if he had nothing to talk with us.

His sudden volte-face surprised us; over the last couple of days, we could win over his confidence and beyond the formalities of an interrogation, he freely interacted with us. We felt that rapport had been shattered; thus, our task to make him speak would be tedious.

Meanwhile, he was served with breakfast: a small bowl full of water gruel and pickle, which he was fond of since his arrival at the guest house.

'Hello Mr Nambi, hope you are fine. Please finish the breakfast, and then we will start.' With a smile, I opened the conversation.

But he remained indifferent as if a stranger is trying to intrude into his privacy. I decided to change my approach.

'An experienced scientist like you can never lose hope. How many times you tried your best for a successful PSLV launch mission? This is yet another challenge in your personal life; I hope that you will take it with all seriousness.' I noticed a change of expression on his face.

With eyes fixed on my face, he responded.

'Who said that I was running away from this challenge? It is only the beginning. But I have nothing more to discuss with you people, as I have said everything to your people who didn't allow me to close my eyes for a second yesterday night.' I could feel a sense of sarcasm in his words.

'That is really great, but you see that these two colleagues with me are eager to speak with you.' I used a different tactic to tackle him.

'If you are so particular, I would narrate all what had happened yesterday night.' I felt that he wanted to ventilate his fury against the interrogators who questioned him yesterday night.

'Yes, we are here for the first time; let us also hear your story.' My colleague's comment slightly irritated him.

'This is the problem; whatever I reveal from the bottom of my heart, you people will treat them as story or naked lies.' He finished his breakfast, showed the empty bowl and continued.

'If I continue to scuff the bottom of the bowl with this spoon, can you expect any more gruel? No.' He placed the bowl and spoon beneath the table and continued.

'This is the way that you people are treating me, I have divulged everything that I know, but you are not satisfied. You are interested to get my disclosures on suggested lines. Yesterday's entire exercise was on that direction and they finally succeeded. I too was saved from further torture and humiliation.'

He paused for a moment and watched our response.

'We cannot decipher your analogies and monologues. Can you tell in plain language as what is in your mind?' I purposefully showed my displeasure on his narrations.

'Sir, simple thing, finally I was convinced of the futility of cooking up all stories. I let out the truth, the true confession by a traitor!' There was a mischievous smile on his face.

'Perhaps you too may be interested to extract such a confession; obviously there is a rat race among you people to take credit out of such professional achievements. I will not disappoint you.'

'Mr Nambi, you are mistaken. We are not the part of any such game; we want to get the truth out of this exercise. You can take it for granted.' I tried to regain his confidence through emotionally surcharged words and phrases.

'But I don't want to retract from my confession that is full of myth and imagination; just like a blockbuster espionage story!' He appeared to be in a lighter vein and strongly desired to share his confession story.

'Everything started when Habibullah Khan came to my residence during 1982 to discuss a business deal, as directed by my schoolmate Abu Baker of Trivandrum. Khan was ready to strike a deal for ₹75 lakh, if I supplied the drawings of Vikas Engine, which were meant for Indonesia. The mediator was Baker. After the visit, I contacted Baker over phone and struck the deal.' Just like a kindergarten kid, he was lucidly narrating the story.

'Who is this Habibullah Khan?' My co-interrogator raised his doubts.

'According to them, he is a Hyderabad-based exporter having business interests in Mumbai, Colombo and other places', he clarified the point.

I was convinced that he is the one among the many characters disclosed by the accused Chandrasekharan during his interrogation. But I kept silent and keenly listened to his narration.

'Our telephone conversation was overheard by one of the operators who incidentally was the wife of my close friend, Sundrarajan. Later, he visited me and informed about this, as a result of which I decided not to proceed with the deal.'

I felt as how ingeniously a natural cover story was framed with all logical ingredients of espionage. But the big question was whether it came out of the imagination of Nambi or someone else?

'But Abu Baker again contacted me during January 1990 and pressed for the deal. Meanwhile, Habibullah Khan also arrived in Trivandrum. They arranged a meeting at Kovalam Hotel, where Sasi and Chandrasekharan were also present. Finally, the deal was struck for ₹1.5 crore. Accordingly, we had to arrange for the delivery of Vikas Engine drawings in three lots, of which two lots were delivered to Fauzia in Trivandrum, whereas the third instalment was scheduled for delivery during the first week of December 1994. A payment of ₹75 lakh in US dollars was made to us during the meeting at Kovalam.'

He expanded the espionage network with more characters.

'During February 1993, when GK delegation from Russia visited Trivandrum, Chandrasekharan who accompanied them met Fauzia at Fort Manor Hotel, Trivandrum, and discussed the proposed visit of Ahmed Pasha of Pakistan. Accordingly, we met Pasha at Fort Manor Hotel during October 1993 and the deal was confirmed for the transfer of cryogenic technology on a payment of US$0.1 million. Initial transfer of documents was through Fauzia.'

Nambi concluded his story with mischievous smile.

Once the names of Habibullah Khan and Ahmed Pasha figured in his confession story, I felt that the cat is now out of the bag. There was no need of any astrologer or soothsayer to ascertain how these names prominently figured in the interrogation statement of the accused. Obviously, these were the names that have been going round in the records of various agencies since long for their dubious role in building up espionage modules targeting our country.

I kept my cards close to my chest and said, 'Mr Nambi, I don't think that you have out smarted the interrogators; after all any confession by an accused is an admission of guilt. The interrogators can easily build up evidence based on your revelations, fictitious or otherwise.'

'That I know well, but the entire framework of the story was created by the interrogators; I have added more flesh and blood to that story to make it more convincing and appealing.' When he came out with the real truth, we virtually were cornered. Then, tactfully we switched over to some grey areas of the espionage story.

'Ok, that means you are an expert in weaving convincing stories. What was the motive in cooking up such a story regarding your decision to quit ISRO in August 1994, at a time when you were heading one of the most prestigious projects? Whether it was due to your fear of exposure or something else?'

I purposefully put the query to corner him, but he came unscathed with convincing reply.

'Two factors mainly influenced my decision. The first one was my personal issues, especially the search for a job for my son. The second factor was the change in Russian contract that had adversely affected our project in ISRO. Even the then director, ISRO was fully aware of these matters as early as in July–August 1994. The so-called espionage scandal had nothing to do with my decision to quit the job in ISRO. Moreover, I submitted my voluntary retirement papers on 1 November 1994 to the director, LPSC, who forwarded it to the chairman, ISRO, on 3 November 1994.'

I saw an air of confidence on his face.

'That may be correct, but certainly there may be some individuals who might have influenced you in taking such a decision.' It was the turn of the co-interrogator.

'I would not deny the fact that my interaction with a couple of good individuals had some impact on my decision. One such person was Kurian of Trivandrum. I came into contact with him in 1992 in connection with the purchase of a disputed property in the heart of Trivandrum city. I advised him not to proceed with the transaction, as one of the parties in the dispute close to me gave all the complex details of that property. Kurian who was probably thankful to me for the advice continued to contact me and thus our friendship developed.

As I was contemplating to seek voluntary retirement from ISRO, I was also looking for a financially sound person for whom I can work after retirement. Kurian who was then heading a construction company mainly dealing with Konkan Railway had plans to expand his ventures into other areas such as aquaculture, shrimp hatchery, mineral water bottling and pineapple processing in which my services were sought for undertaking project viability analysis.'

He was trying to justify his decision to quit ISRO.

'That means, while heading major projects in ISRO, you were engaged in other private assignments for profit? We cannot rule out the possibility of Mr Kurian using you as an intermediary to make inroads into ISRO with his new ventures, isn't it?' I interrupted his narration.

'I was assisting Kurian without affecting my duties or tasks in ISRO. He had met my travel expenses for my journey to different places in connection with his business. Similarly, he also met the telephone expenses of my residential phone which was used for making domestic and overseas calls for such purposes. Since

February 1994, my son was employed as computer operator in his establishment. Besides, he has given my son a loan of around ₹3 lakh for launching LPG distribution agency. I can say for certain that Kurian has done these things not out of his plan to use me as an intermediary to launch his ventures in ISRO. Instead, he was interested to induct me into his projects after my retirement.'

Nambi tried to justify his association with the business group purely on personal level.

'You told that you were in communication with overseas bodies and firms in connection with Kurian's projects. Which were these bodies and what was the nature of interaction?' One of the co-interrogators confronted him with his natural query.

'Apart from assisting Kurian in his domestic projects, I used to help him in preparing global tenders for supply of materials connected with civil constructions. One such major tender was the pile foundation works of Manila Port floated by the government of the Philippines. This project was designed by an Australian government company at Victoria. As part of the project, I was in communication with the technical and other experts of these projects in Manila and Victoria. I accompanied him to Manila for further negotiation and finalization of the contract. We stayed in Manila for around three days and returned to Madras via Kuala Lumpur. Kurian paid the flight and travel expenses. I took formal permission from the director, LPSC, for these visits.'

He stood his ground that his visit and other activities outside ISRO were within the knowledge of ISRO authorities.

'Whether you have tried to use these foreign trips to explore prospective buyers of ISRO developed technology, especially the Viking and cryogenic engines technology?' I posed this question to ascertain his foreign contacts.

Answering our question, Nambi explained in detail the various technical and scientific aspects connected with Viking and cryogenic technologies.

'There is much confusion and ambiguities in such matters. Even I am surprised that some of the interrogators are ignorant of the difference between a rocket and missile. We have developed Viking technology on the basis of French technology. The developed countries such as the USA, Russia, China, France and Japan have technology superior to our Viking technology. On the other hand, developing countries such as Pakistan, Indonesia and Brazil do not have the required infrastructure to indigenously develop this technology. Thus, even if any of these countries clandestinely procure technology drawings or design, they will be unable to develop this technology for want of infrastructure which includes liquid propellant handling/storage facilities and above all the production of the propellant. Many of these countries have the required infrastructure for solid propulsion system. For example, Pakistan has a solid rocket "Sherkhan" which is indigenously developed by using the borrowed technology from France.

On the question of transfer of cryogenic engine technology, India does not have the complete technology and no country would venture to buy such half-baked technology from India. Further, developed countries which are in possession of this technology are not interested in buying the Russian technology, as they do not have the pedigree or wherewithal for this particular technology. Equally obnoxious is the claim that some hostile countries like Pakistan are interested to procure this technology for defence purpose. No missile using cryogenic propulsion system is developed in any part of the world, because of the simple fact that any missile using this technology needs longer preparation time, which is not at all viable in defence strategies.

Regarding the sale of ISRO-developed technology, there is an autonomous body, namely Antrix Corporation, to promote the transfer/sale of technology and hardware within India and abroad. Delegates from any country interested in buying such technology can visit the concerned ISRO unit where presentation has been arranged for them with the permission of ISRO headquarters. I along with other ISRO scientists have made two such presentations to the delegations from China and Brazil. Teams from other countries like the USA have also paid visit to ISRO centres in this regard. Thus, the allegation that I used my visits abroad to find prospective buyers for ISRO-developed technology is baseless.'

Nambi concluded his technical dissertation to enlighten us.

'Are there any other bodies or firms engaged in promoting the sale of ISRO developed technology?' I wanted to elicit some inputs about the firms allegedly involved in the case.

'Obviously, I know that you are targeting two establishments on which a lot of rumours are now in the air. The first one is MTAR of Hyderabad whose key functionary Ravindra Reddy is close to the PM's son Prabhakar Rao. I know Reddy since the mid-1980s. During 1986–1987, ISRO had awarded contract to MTAR for the fabrication of Vikas Engine. The Contract Negotiation Committee headed by Mr Varadan, the then joint secretary, Department of Space, in which I was also a member, followed the due procedures in awarding the contract. There was nothing unusual in this contract, as ISRO usually awarded contracts to leading firms for fabrication works.

The other firm which is in news is HEI whose officials on some occasions accompany the personnel of ASC of France during visit to ISRO. As far as my information goes, ISRO had directly dealt with ASC in launching our satellites. At the same time, I cannot say for certain whether HEI has some liaison role for which they receive any commission from ASC or not.'

'Which are the other agencies or individuals in receipt of commissions from ISRO for such liaison or other tasks?' My co-interrogator raised the question.

'ISRO regularly makes payments to GK for technology transfer/consultancy. I am not aware of the quantum of payment. The transactions are made through Bank of Rajasthan. More details are not known to me as such matters are dealt by the financial controller and his department. Chandrasekharan being in the capacity of the liaison man of GK was in receipt of the commission from the Russian agency. He is close to Alexi Vasin of GK.'

Nambi felt exhausted due to the lengthy narration of the story. My colleague interrogators also left for lunch.

Left alone, Nambi revealed that his confession before the interrogators was nothing but a story meant to please the interrogators. He reiterated that never in his life, he had seen the Maldivian ladies; nor he mentioned the name of IGP Raman Srivastava as linked to the espionage. When the interrogators and investigators fabricated characters or events to strengthen their espionage story, he too had woven such a story of confession. Before leaving the interrogation room, I shared a few words of caution: 'Don't succumb, keep telling the truth. Truth cannot be covered for long; once your innocence would be established.'

Just like Pontius Pilate was convinced of the innocence of Jesus Christ, I too was sure that this scientist was innocent. But I was helpless to utter this truth so long as I remained behind the iron wall of a secret organization. And outside, there was a frenzied mob—just like high priests and Jews—clamouring for the blood of innocent scientists and others!

CAUGHT BY THE RED HANDS OF JUDICIARY

11

Once the CBI had taken over the investigation of the case on 3 December 1994, the venue of the ISRO spy story was shifted to central Kerala when the different stakeholders of the case knocked at the doors of judiciary with their exaggerated claims and counterclaims. My colleague there had a hectic time liaising and briefing the new team of investigators including the CBI sleuths to toe the line of espionage already built up by various agencies. Very often, his ego prompted him to share the great things that he had been engaged in for the senior bosses.

The sole three-star hotel in the city cut off from the mainland and located at the island named after Lord Wellington was the main rendezvous of senior officers and personnel. There was no dearth of funds or resources to meet all these expenses. After all, it was the life and death struggle of the great Bengali Dada of the Bureau in New Delhi to demolish the first major spy network in South India so that his pending application with higher echelons, for the change of date of birth in service records, would be favourably settled before his impending superannuation!

Our liaison man was apparently unhappy with the approach of the CBI officer in charge of investigation, who was not ready to swallow all what the initial investigators/agencies had fed to him. Thus, signals to this effect had gone to the senior bosses who arranged a high level meeting at the state capital in which the head of the SIT of the Kerala Police, in the presence of other senior bosses, presented a fascinating story of espionage, which too was not taken seriously by the CBI officer. Then the move was to dislodge him from that assignment. Thanks to the then director of CBI, who had successfully countered such moves. Perhaps, his uncompromising approach invited unsavoury references even from the seats of justice!

As legal battles connected with the ISRO espionage case were in the offing, the centre of attraction was the visiting legal luminaries from New Delhi and elsewhere. Many among them were keen to enjoy the scenic beauty of the state and other facilities; a reputed legal expert from the capital was keener to leisurely spending hours on the sprawling lawns of the hotel facing the backwaters, sipping different brands of foreign liquor. In such a euphoric mood, sometimes, he batted both for the batting and bowling teams!

While the CBI investigators showed reservations to endorse the espionage line obviously due to lack of any specific evidence as attributed by the initial investigators and agencies, a set of political leaders and police officers from behind the curtain used the legal fraternity to steer off the case in pursuance of their ulterior motives. It was at a time when the image building exercise in Congress-led ruling alliance in the state was gaining momentum and the clamour for the removal of the leader had reached high pitch and echoed at the corridors of power in New Delhi. Ironically, all forces within the party and those elements and groups disguised as human rights protagonists or ultra-left activists having historical enmity towards the leader rallied together to unseat him from power. They could well exploit the spicy espionage story to their advantage by using the sections of the media that had built up so much hype that the people in the street had virtually treated the accused of the case as traitors. The catchy slogans 'Sack Srivastava' and 'Resign Karunakaran' filled the air in every nook and corner of the state. Such mass psyche and public trial of the accused had even influenced sections of judiciary.

Thus, no one was astonished when Cochin-based Niyamavedi (lawyers' forum)—a public spirited organization comprising lawyers and activists moved—Kerala High Court[1] inter alia praying for the issuance of a writ of mandamus directing the director of CBI, New Delhi, to arrest Raman Srivastava, IPS, IGP, southern zone, Kerala state for his alleged involvement in the ISRO espionage case and for a direction to the state of Kerala to suspend and remove him from service. Naturally, the single judge of the high court dismissed the petition with the observation that the power of interference of the court in the subject in hand at that stage was very limited. It also recorded that statement of the state government to the effect that the government had no interest in unduly defending or shielding any officer and that the government would proceed in the matter only when report from the CBI, which is investigating in the case, is received.

In an appeal[2] filed on 21 December 1994, a division bench of the Kerala High Court, after a detailed judgement, dismissed the case on 13 January 1995, holding that no court has power to direct the investigating officer (IO) to include a person as an accused in the case while the investigation is in progress. But what surprised legal experts were the certain observations made by the division bench. Instead of outrightly dismissing the petition which was based on print media reports and gossips, uncorroborated interrogation statements and electronic evidences produced by the investigators, the court had elaborately discussed the significance of public interest litigations (PILs) and the role of the fourth estate in democracy.

Ironically, the court passed unusually critical observation on the CBI investigations despite the fact that the agency had only initiated the investigation. The bench observed:

> [S]ince we were not satisfied with the affidavits filed by the abovementioned officers (CBI), we directed Sri Vijaya Rama Rao, the

. . . .

[1] O. P. 17367 of 1994 dated 13 December 1994 represented by its member K. Nandini vs Raman Srivastava (IPS Inspector General of Police).
[2] W. A. No. 1676 of 1994-C dated 21 December 1994 of Kerala High Court (1995 CriLJ 1976).

Director of Central Bureau of Investigation, to peruse the entire records and to satisfy himself as to whether the investigation is proceeding in the proper line. His conclusions, on such examination, were to be submitted to Court in the form of an affidavit.[3]

In fact, some of the findings/observations of the bench had given new dimensions to the ISRO espionage case. For example, while the bench cast doubts on the CBI investigation, they had attached much sacrosanct to the electronic evidence such as video cassettes produced by the other agencies on the confession statements of the accused like Fauzia, Chandrasekharan and Sasikumaran without ascertaining the manner how such cassettes were produced or their authenticity. In this regard, the observations made by the court assume much significance.

When Fousiya, Chandrasekharan and Sashikumar were questioned by the Intelligence Bureau (IB), the same was recorded in Video Cassettes. The three Video Cassettes produced before the Court by the IB were viewed by us by playing it in a Video Cassette Player belonging to this court. From that it is crystal clear that these three accused gave answers to the questions without any fear or torture. They were seen in very jovial and calm mood, free from any stress or strain. So the answers given by the accused at the time of questioning had never be considered as the result of any torture by the police and for that matter any authority.[4]

No doubt, the courts have absolute powers to call for any piece of evidence—physical, electronic or otherwise—but the heart of the matter is that no court upholding true traditions of justice would make any observations or reach any conclusive decisions on the basis of uncorroborated electronic evidence. In the instant case, had the division bench taken more objective and judicious approach in evaluating such electronic evidences, they would have

. . . .

[3] Ibid (https://indiankanoon.org/doc/1232603/?type=print accessed on 24 January 2019).
[4] Ibid.

avoided the critical observations and directions, which no doubt had prevented the subsequent executive actions to establish an espionage case which really didn't exist. And finally a number of innocent souls might have been saved from the tragic ordeal, humiliation and sufferings. Perhaps the words of Fauzia, immediately after her acquittal by the apex court, threw much light to such truth.

> They (Interrogators) also gave me a statement and brought in a video-camera. Because of the threat to my daughter, I said that I had brought money and gave it to Sasikumaran. If you see the video, you can see that I keep hesitating because that I did not know the names of Srivastava and Nambi Narayanan. They had written the names on a piece of paper and I had to keep wearing my spectacles to read. Because of that, there are many cuts in the video.[5]

Ironically, the legal luminaries who meticulously analysed the video cassettes before reaching their crucial conclusions could not show the sagacity and acumen of this semi-literate lady!

The observations made by the apex court on 6 April 1995[6] while disposing a special leave petition filed by the director, CBI, and others against the appellate order of the division bench point towards this reality.

> The petitioners had, as directed by the Division Bench, produced for perusal of the Court case diaries of the Kerala State Police as well as of the C.B.I. relating to the investigations carried out in respect of the said crimes including the statements recorded in the course of investigation and certain video cassettes in that connection. These were perused by the Division Bench in chambers. However, a reference at some length has been made in the course of the judgment to the material disclosed in the course of

....
[5] Ritu Sarin, 'Victims Not Spies', *The Indian Express* (1996, 17 March).
[6] Director, CBI vs Niyamavedi & others. Special Leave Petition (crl.) 942 of 1995 (1995 (3) SCR 196).

investigation, presumably, in order to examine the contention relating to the alleged involvement of the first respondent in the crimes in question. Clearly, under the Code of Criminal Procedure, 1973, only a very limited use can be made of the statements to the police and police diaries, even in the course of the trial, as set out in Sections 162 and 172 of the Code of Criminal Procedure. The Division Bench, therefore, should have refrained from disclosing in its order, material contained in these diaries and statements, especially when the investigation in the very case was in progress. It should also have refrained from making any comments on the manner in which investigation was being conducted by the C.B.I., looking to the fact that the investigation was far from complete.

The question that haunts many of us, as rightly pointed out by the SC, is how the bench had gone beyond its legal boundaries and made sweeping observations against a premier investigation agency which was engaged in the investigation of a sensational case? As it relates to the matters of judiciary, I feel it inappropriate to openly discuss such questions.

Such questions and doubts on the approach of judiciary had come up among legal circles in respect of other ISRO espionage-related cases. These cases mainly pertained to the legality of the closure report submitted by the CBI and the move of the state government to reopen and reinvestigate the case. The investigation of the case initially carried out by the Kerala Police was taken over by CBI on 3 December 1994[7] at the request of the state of Kerala.[8] Consequently, cases RC 10(S)/94 and RC and RC 11(S)/94[9] were registered in SIC II Branch of the CBI. On completion of

....

[7] Vide DPCT Notification No. 228/ST/94-AVD-II (1&2) dated 2 December 1994.
[8] Notification of the Home Department, Kerala, notification no. 66329/SSA 3/94/Home, dated 2 December 1994.
[9] Case No. RC 10(S)/94 U/S 14 of Foreigners Act & Para 7 of Foreigners Act, 1948 (Case Cr No. 225/94) and Case No. RC 11 (S)/U/S 120B R/W Section 3.4.&5 of Official Secrets Act r/w Section 34 of IPC (Case No. 226/94) dated 3 December 1994.

investigation in RC 10(S)/94, a charge sheet had been filed before the Chief Judicial Magistrate (CJM), Ernakulum, Kerala on 17 December 1994 with detailed reasons and unambiguous grounds. A crucial part of the aforementioned report explained:

'Thus, it would be seen that the statements of the accused recorded by the Kerala Police are mutually contradictory within themselves and similarly the statements recorded by IB are mutually contradictory and above all the statements of IB and Kerala Police are contradictory.' One of the main conclusions of the CBI was 'during the investigation neither any evidence came on record indicating that the accused indulged in espionage activities by way of passing on of secret documents of ISRO or any of the Defence Establishments nor any incriminating documents could be recovered.'[10]

Ironically, a spate of petitions was filed before the single bench of Kerala High Court by lawyers, police officers and those not connected with the case against CBI's closure report and the 2 May 1996 order of the CJM of Ernakulum discharging all the six accused in the case and accepting the CBI's closure report.[11] All the petitioners questioned the CBI's closure of the case on three counts: loose ends remained to be tied up despite the CBI'S investigation; the CJM had committed a grave error in not issuing notice to the first informant before dropping the proceedings under Sections 173 of the CrPC and there was dishonest intention on the CBI's part to help the accused.[12] The court, while dismissing all these petitions except that of S. Vijayan, deputy superintendent of police (DSP), who initially registered the case against Maldivian ladies on the grounds of visa violations, stayed the order of CJM on 18 July 1996.

....

[10] S. Nambi Narayanan vs Siby Mathews & Others. Civil Appeal Nos. 6637–6638 of 2018, SC, dated 14 September 2018 (https://indiankanoon.org/doc/140150087/ accessed on 24 January 2019).
[11] Palani R. Swamy, 'No End in Sight', *Outlook* (1996, 7 August).
[12] S. Nambi Narayanan vs Siby Mathews & Others.

While admitting petition of Vijayan on technical grounds, the court ordered to issue notices to all respondents with the decision that legality, propriety and other matters would be decided on the merits of the case and the court would examine whether the CJM has properly applied his mind in accepting the closure report. The main fact in issue before the court was whether the petitioner was entitled to be the first informant within the purview of Section 154 of the CrPC and as such has the privilege to get a notice of the CJM's order. Though the CBI contended that he is not the first informant, advocate general of the state submitted otherwise. The leading lawyer of the SC, Ram Jethmalani, who appeared on behalf of the petitioner had contended that the CBI was engaged in a cover-up operation and they had not gone into the available evidence like the links of senior ISRO scientist with Malé women and the meeting of Mariam Rasheeda with Dr Anand Saldanha at Calicut Railway Station, etc. As the court was convinced of the stand of CBI, it dismissed the petition on 27 November 1996.

Earlier in May 1996, V. S. Achuthanandan, former CM and senior leader of the Communist Party of India (Marxist) (CPI[M]) moved the high court,[13] asking for a judicial probe into the ISRO case. The court rejected the plea holding that the judicial probe is not an alternative to investigation and made an observation that if the state desires, it can reopen and reinvestigate the case.

Meanwhile, on 19 June 1996, the Kerala government took decision to reinvestigate[14] the case and to cancel the order empowering CBI to investigate the case. The assistance of IB and Research and Analysis Wing (RAW) was also sought for. A new team headed by C. A. Chali, IPS, was tipped off, while T. P. Senkumar, IPS, was promoted and posted as DIG (Crime) with the task of directly reinvestigating the case. The state government issued another notification on July 1996, which, in fact, euphemistically redefined the

....

[13] V. S. Achuthanandan vs State of Kerala (OP. No. 5128 of 1996 decided on 27 May 1996).
[14] Notification No. 27707/SSA -3/96/Home, dated 27 June 1996 (published as Extraordinary Gazette No. 823 dated 6 July 1996).

probe as a further investigation into the spy case rather than a reinvestigation. The change in terms has been adopted to avoid legal complications arising out of initiating a reinvestigation when the CBI has already completed an investigation.

Though such legal ambiguities and loopholes were aplenty on the government's decision, ironically the august institutions of judiciary in the state, perhaps influenced by the mass psyche, gave the green signal to go ahead with the reinvestigation or further investigation after completing the formalities. Thus, while dismissing the writ petitions filed by the accused against the State government decision to reopen the case, the Kerala High Court consisting of Justice K. G. Balakrishnan and B. N. Patnaik on 27 November 1996 held that the state government can proceed for further investigation of the case with a formal permission from CJM Ernakulum before whom the CBI filed the closure report discharging all the accused. The court maintained that as the CBI's report having been accepted by the CJM, there can be no dispute under section 178(8) of the CrPC, the police is empowered to file an additional report against the accused in the event of additional material evidence comes to their notice on further investigation.

Similarly on 13 December 1996, CJM Trivandrum, while disposing the plea of DIG T. P. Senkumar to reopen the case, dismissed the objection of CBI and three accused (Mariam, Fauzia and Sasikumaran) that CJM was not competent to decide the case under the Official Secrets Act, 1923. Referring to the order of CJM Ernakulum on CBI's closure report, the CJM observed that it was only an order of discharge and not of acquittal of the accused and a new probe did not infringe on the rights of the accused. 'It was open for the investigation agency to collect more reliable evidence and submit a final report, though the closure report submitted by CBI was accepted by the court.'

But the apex court[15] had cleared such legal ambiguities and interpretations through their historic judgement on 29 April 1998.

---

[15] K. Chandrasekhar, Mariam ... vs The State Of Kerala & Ors, Supreme Court of India (Special Leave petition (Crl.) No. 593 of 1998).

The bench consisting of Justices M. K. Mukherjee and Syed Shah Mohammed Quadri categorically stated that the decision of the Kerala government to withdraw the consent for investigation it had given to the CBI (after the central agency had completed its investigation and a court had ordered the release of the accused) and to entrust the case back with the Kerala Police for further investigation was 'patently invalid and unsustainable in law' and could only be considered as a 'mala fide exercise of power'.

Pointing out that the duty of an investigating agency is not to bolster a prosecution case with such evidence as would bring about a conviction but to bring out the unvarnished truth, the court said, in its most damning conclusion:

> ...the Kerala Government wants the instant case to be further investigated by a team nominated by it with the avowed object of establishing that the accused are guilty, even after the investigating agency of its choice, the CBI, found that no case had been made out against them.

It is said that it was 'undoubtedly a matter of concern and consternation' that the government had issued a notification for another investigation, which does not 'comport with the known pattern of a responsible Government bound by rule of law'. The apex court concluded cryptically by saying that 'we say no more' and ordered the state government to pay ₹1 lakh to each of the six accused as costs.

Though the SC, through this judgement, put the final seal on the ongoing litigations on the ISRO case, the perpetrators of the ISRO tragedy—on their own or through their vexatious litigants—tried to white wash the entire episode, highlighting the crucial aspects of the national security and related issues. However, the victims, notably scientist Nambi Narayanan, relentlessly fought to ensure victims' rights and public justice.

From the beginning of ISRO espionage case, there were organized efforts to silence the media personnel and independent intellectuals who grasped the real truth and tried to counter the imaginary espionage story. Conscious efforts were made to discredit them through disinformation and malicious campaign linking them with various foreign agencies and media tycoons. Side by side, a series of defamation suits were filed by the involved police officers or the public interest litigants and others sponsored by them.

Siby Mathews, IPS, who conducted the initial inquiry in the case filed a complaint against Chennai-based fortnightly *The Frontline* for publishing an article 'A Witch Hunt Ends'[16] in May 1996, stating that it contained 'scandalous imputations which harmed the reputation of the Kerala Police before the eye of the public', 'lowered its dignity' and affected its 'morale' and therefore sought remedy for defamation. Even novel methods apparently meant to influence the judiciary have been resorted to by the petitioner. Thus, a senior income tax commissioner who absolutely had no locus standi in the case disposed before the court and testified that he knew the DIG for 28 years known for his integrity and honesty. Based on petitions filed subsequently by N. Ram,[17] the editor of *The Frontline* and others, the Kerala High Court on 23 March 2000 quashed the complaint holding that the words or the passages found in the article would not constitute offences punishable under Sections 500 (punishment for defamation). Similar defamation cases by others against the print and electronic channels like the Asianet and *India Today* also met with the same fate. However, these defamation cases dragged on for two to three years.

Where the fox kept playing under sheep's skin, the real victims of ISRO espionage case were left in the dark. Disposing such complaints in turn led to an inordinate delay, creating impediments in the speedy dispensation of justice. The Maldivian ladies Mariam Rasheeda and Fauzia became the forsaken casualties of such delay. While the other accused were released after the

....
[16] T. S. Subramanyam, 'A Witch Hunt Ends', *Frontline* (1996, 31 May).
[17] N. Ram vs Siby Mathew and Anr. on 23 March 2000 (citations: 2000 CriLJ 3118).

acceptance of the CBI's report by the CJM, Ernakulum, the ordeal of these ladies continued, with the state police refusing, under one pretext or the other, to allow them to leave the country. A couple of defamation cases filed against them by police and others for alleged statements made by them before the print and electronic media about the conduct of certain police officers had resulted in their continued incarceration. In the case of Fauzia, charges were later framed against her under the National Security Act[18] (NSA) prolonging her detention.

However, such strategies did not deter the indomitable spirit of Nambi Narayanan to continue his legal crusade. He approached the National Human Rights Commission (NHRC) in 1995. In its 6 September 1996 ruling, NHRC, on the basis of their finding that there was 'gross violation of human rights of the complainant by officers of Kerala police and the IB' ordered the Kerala government to release a compensation of ₹10 lakh to him as interim compensation. It also advised the Union Home Ministry to hold an enquiry to identify the officials who had committed the excesses and also favoured appropriate disciplinary and criminal action against them. However, the centre and state government raised objections saying that the award can affect the outcome of the civil suit filed by him claiming damages amounting to ₹1 crore from the erred officials. The state government also continued the witch-hunt and obtained a stay on the NHRC order from the high court, which was vacated on 7 September 2012.

Perhaps the most significant of all the legal cases connected with ISRO case is the ongoing legal battle spanning over a decade, against those Kerala Police officials who initially investigated the case. In April 1996, the CBI sent a report to the state government 'on the role of certain officials of Kerala Police in the investigation of ISRO espionage case'. The CBI's recommendation to initiate appropriate action against the erred officials was placed for a

....

[18] Kerala government issued special orders on 12 December 1996 to arrest her under NSA in view of pending defamation cases.

decision before the then CM E. K. Nayanar in December 1997. Though the State Home Department favoured rejecting the recommendation, Nayanar disagreed with their finding and made a separate note dated 12 December 1997 which said: 'decision (on whether to take action against the officers or not) may be taken up on receipt of the Supreme Court judgement' that was pending in a related case. The SC disposed that case on 29 April 1998 acquitting all the accused and directing the state government to pay ₹1 lakh to each of the six accused. Despite the SC judgement, Nayanar's note was kept in cold storage for more than one decade.

The first agenda of the Oommen Chandy-led Congress government, on assuming office, was to give an ignominious burial to the aforementioned note through an order dated 29 June 2011. There was nothing astonishing in issuing such an order as the Congress faction led by Chandy was most benefitted out of the ISRO espionage case. But the reason ascribed to dropping the charges against the officials in the summing up paragraph of the order is as follows:

> Governments are of the view that it is not proper or legal to take disciplinary action against the officials for the alleged lapses pointed out in the investigation report of the CBI at this juncture, after the lapse of 15 years and therefore Government decide that no disciplinary action need be taken against the above officials for their alleged lapses in the investigation of the ISRO case.[19]

That government order was challenged by Nambi Narayanan and others during 2012 in Kerala High Court which quashed the order and directed the government to take action in a just and legal manner. Accepting the judgement, the state government formed a committee to take action. But the erring officials filed writ appeal before a division bench of Kerala High Court, which

....

[19] Nambi Narayanan vs Siby Mathews & Others Etc., SC (Civil Appeal Nos. 6637–6638 of 2018).

on 4 March 2015 set aside the judgement of the single judge. The division bench, while holding that no action was required against the erred officials after a lapse of 15 years, observed that 'the report of the CBI was only an opinion; the Government may consider or may not consider such opinion'. Nambi Narayanan's appeal against the judgement of the division bench is now pending in the SC.

The issues raised by Nambi Narayanan in the aforementioned appeal in the apex court assume considerable importance on many grounds. First, all the three agencies, namely Kerala Police, the IB and the CBI, associated with the ISRO espionage case came under shadow of doubt and criticisms, adversely affecting their professional image and reputation. The criticism against the police was that the internal politics in the force coupled with their vested political interest compelled the agency to negate the very concept of the due process of law during the investigations. No less than an officer of the rank of additional director general of police (ADGP) had written a letter to the then director general of police (DGP) of Kerala alleging that confessions were extracted from the accused to falsely implicate Raman Srivastava, the then IGP, who maintained good relations with the Congress leader K. Karunakaran. Similarly, the IB has come under scanner for their lack of professionalism, whereas CBI was targeted by sections of media and erred police officials for their alleged cover-up during investigations. Thus, the decision of the SC on 14 September 2018, directing the state of Kerala to pay a compensation of ₹50 lakh to Nambi Narayanan in lieu of the acts of omissions and commissions from the part of the state super structures and ordering the constitution of a committee for obtaining factual scenario that led to the arrest of Nambi Narayanan, in many respects, has set right these issues by fixing responsibility over officials or agencies for their omissions and commissions.

The decision would send a clear message to all concerned agencies that the offences against public justice are punishable under Section 340 of the CrPC. This would help to create deterrence among the personnel against succumbing to unlawful or illegal actions adversely affecting the image and integrity of those agencies. The concept of public justice now transcends beyond the conventional spheres and is inextricably intertwined with development and welfare of any modern society. The heart of the matter is that the lack of professionalism and the failure of state institutions retard the process of development and the onward march of the nation to progress and prosperity. The cases such as ISRO espionage create negative impact. For example, demoralization of scientists and scientific community can derail or slow down the advancements in the field of science and technology, especially the area of space technology. Already it is a known fact that the ISRO espionage case has delayed India's ambitious cryogenic engine project by more than 15 years. Similarly, the mounting campaign and propaganda by the vested interests that the rule of law and due process of law are in jeopardy could be checkmated to a great extent through the apex court decision.

Finally, the SC judgement has opened broader issues such as the proper streamlining of the law enforcement and security–investigation organizations by ensuring accountability, transparency and professionalism through statutory or other mechanisms. They should uphold the guidelines of the arrest/detention and the concept of due process of law so that illegal arrest and incarceration of innocent victims, that eat away their body, mind and reputation, can be avoided.

As rightly commented by Anthony Glees[20]:

> [T]he issues such as the political accountability and oversight of secret intelligence agencies, their accountability and competence in terms of tradecraft, professional skills and ethical values have emerged as major theme of debate in many countries like United

---

[20] Anthony Glees, 'The Future of Intelligence Studies', *Journal of Strategic Security* 6, no. 3 (2013). Available at https://scholarcommons.usf.edu/jss/vol6/iss5/15/ (accessed on 24 January 2019).

Kingdom. Glees noted that the UK currently faces big problems in respect of making covert action accountable.

Such debates had come up in India too, especially in the wake of major intelligence failures and internal security challenges. Though a private bill, namely the Intelligence Services (Powers and Regulation) Bill, 2011,[21] was slated for discussion in the parliament to ensure the accountability of the functioning of intelligence agencies in the country, the aforementioned bill had not seen the light of the day. In democracies like India, where the transparency and accountability of state super structures have become the facets of democracy, such legislations and reforms are crucial in maintaining the image and reputation of these agencies.

---

[21] https://timesofindia.indiatimes.com/india/Manish-Tewaris-Bill-sought-to-regulate-IB-RAW-NTROs-operations/articleshow/21134566.cms (accessed on 24 January 2019).

POLITICS THAT IGNITED THE FIRE

12

On the late night of 14 February 1995, I received an urgent call from the state Bureau chief. From the other end, I heard his feeble voice.

'You know that the demand for the removal of leader from the CM's post has gained further momentum. The ball is now in the court of the PM, who is keen to ascertain the exact line of approach of front partners. There are different claims on the stand of the league party. Our chief has to furnish a concrete report on the issue. The PM desires to have a personal interaction with the supremo of league party to ascertain their line. We will make all the travel arrangements. You know that it is an urgent task.'

I sensed a tone of anxiety and concern in his voice.

His words had really puzzled me. No doubt, I have good rapport with the supremo, who really was a simpleton not much conversant with the Machiavellian politics. The big question was 'to be or not to be': Whether he would agree to our suggestion for a trip to Delhi to meet the PM, especially at a time when the political situation in the state remained surcharged with the growing demand for the resignation of the CM.

'Sir, as you are aware, he is only the figure head of the party; all crucial decisions are taken by the party's minister handling key portfolios. Our suggestion for the visit would be definitely discussed with the minister and others. Whether they would endorse it or not is a different question, but the key issue is how we will maintain its secrecy. The print media is always after these leaders.'

I tried to explain the inherent difficulties.

'As executive officers, we should overcome such hurdles. We should make use of our good rapport with him; convince him that it is a secret mission as desired by the PM. After all, he is getting an invitation from the head of the nation for a personal meeting! If you properly handle the task, I am sure he will not make any objection to our proposal. Time is short; do everything fast.'

The chief was quite impatient and was in no mood to prolong the discussions.

For me, it was a sleepless night. Many questions churned up in my mind: How should I convince him of our mission? Whether he would agree or not? How the secrecy could be maintained? If the operation is exposed by his party or the media, what would be my fate? Whether the bosses would shield me or not? Moreover, the very thought that no less a person than the PM of the country is in the picture had made me more tense.

In the whirlpool of such worried thoughts, the various characters and episodes of ISRO espionage case flashed across my mind. It was in the month of November 1994 that a similar call made me associated with the ISRO case, which then was nothing but a visa violation case of two Maldivian women, inflated by the perverted mind of a dubious police officer. Within a short span of three months, it had become the biggest spy story of India, with all the elements of a thriller—spies, a honey trap, politics and foreign intelligence agencies. But the most surprising fact was that this spy story succinctly spun by the shrewd masters had soon emerged as a major political controversy.

The CPI(M)-led Left Democratic Front (LDF) made the story a cause celebre, using it to target the then PM Narasimha Rao and the then Kerala CM K. Karunakaran—the former for the allegations of the involvement of his son Prabhakar Rao and the latter for allegedly shielding Raman Srivastava, then IGP, an accused in the espionage case. The IG, moreover, had become a bête noire of the Communists and certain communal outfits, as early as in December 1991, when a Muslim girl Sirajunisa was killed during police firing in Palakkad district where he had the jurisdictional control as deputy inspector general (DIG) of police. The faction in the state Congress party, instead of resisting such organized campaigns against party's CM Karunakaran, exploited it as a weapon to intensify their moves to ouster him from CM's chair.

The chronic conspiracy theorists—the exponents of rabid nationalism and patriotism—interpreted it as the latest example of the sinister designs of our hostile neighbour to destabilize the nation through covert operations like espionage. In order to make political mileage, they targeted both the Congress and the CPM, alleging that their strategy of vote bank politics by hobnobbing communal and sectarian forces had turned Kerala into a fertile ground of spies, traitors and anti-national forces.

The signs of the emerging political conspiracy had come to the fore even during the initial phase of the interrogation of the key suspects. A beeline of journalists and local politicians of the state capital were after the interrogators and investigating sleuths to get the inside story which they easily moulded up to suit their political or other interests.

The stakes of investigators and police personnel associated with the case had gone high; every Tom, Dick and Harry from top to bottom spoke to the crazy media and political leaders as whatever they thought sound and safe to justify their actions. The political masters could easily exploit their rapport with those officers and personnel; a senior leader of the Congress party who headed the campaign against Karunakaran successfully used such connections to cook up the espionage story on desired lines.

Thus, overnight the stories of Prabhakar Rao and Raman Srivastava had become authentic revelations by the accused! The photograph of Srivastava was rightly identified by the accused Mariam and

Fauzia, who ironically had never seen him in their life! Moreover, such revelations as official reports had reached the desks of MOS (Home), cabinet secretary, home secretary and a whole lot of officials at the highest echelons of power! Even the august institutions of the judiciary attached much sacrosanct to such reports and passed sweeping orders!

The names of Raman Srivastava and Prabhakar Rao which went around every nook and corner of the state and outside linking to ISRO case had not appeared as bolt from the blue. The first indication was that Srivastava's name was hinted by Mariam and Fauzia who confused his identity as Brigadier but subsequently clarified by Chandrasekharan and Dr Sasikumaran. However, in the case of Prabhakar Rao, it was doubly sure that Chandrasekharan first indicated this name along with the names of more than two dozen senior bureaucrats, business tycoons, legal experts and scientists as suspects of the case! Definitely, he wanted to avoid the heat of interrogation by cooking up such names.

One thing was crystal clear; the names of Srivastava and Rao were leaked out by some interrogators or those who handled the case. The unanswered question was what motivated them to do so? But it was beyond doubt that behind the curtain political game shrewdly played by a Congress leader who was subsequently elevated as the CM of the state was the real inspiration for such unethical moves.

My thoughts travelled in a different plane. How such things can happen in professional organizations with ethical code of conduct? Basically, it was the outcome of the unprofessional approach of those who head these professional bodies. Sometimes, dominating personal or career interests to ensure cosy assignments or extension of service after superannuation prompted many of them not to listen to their voice of conscience. Similarly, good personal equation with those who mattered very often influenced their decisions.

In that respect, the personal equation of the leader with a section of higher echelons of such agencies in the state was not as cordial as in the case of a set of senior Congress leaders who always carried the halo of mass leaders created through political gimmicks and self-imposed style of simplicity and populism. From the private conversation and gossips of some of these officers, I could easily make out that leader had consciously avoided them for the so-called interaction and briefing for which his predecessors had great fascination. As a mass leader elevated to the pinnacle of party set up through many decades of historic struggles and agitations, he better assessed the pulse of the masses rather than depending on the hackneyed and half-baked reports or briefings by the bureaucrats.

As astute and experienced as he was, Karunakaran failed to gauge correctly the intensity of the brewing storm of ISRO case or the growing resentment in the state party against him. Perhaps his overconfidence as kingmaker of P. V. Narasimha Rao, as the PM in 1991, after the death of Rajiv Gandhi and his status as a trouble shooter of the party and the most powerful Congress CM, had made him incapable to see the writings on the wall. He could never think of the steady erosion of a number of his protégé loyalists from his camp, alleging leader's eagerness to promote his son as his successor in the state party.

Emboldened by such dynamics on the group alignments in the party, the faction opposed to Karunakaran intensified their revolt against the leader demanding his removal from the leadership of the Congress legislature party. They resorted to horse trading and other unethical means to deprive him of his majority in the legislative party. They had submitted a charge sheet against him with the party high command and demanded his resignation in public meetings across the state, depicting him as a spy and an anti-national. Despite such organized moves for his removal, he stuck to his ground on Srivastava's issue and reiterated that he would complete his five-year term as the CM.

But his overconfidence was short-lived when his foes within the party opened new battlefronts to placate coalition partners. By playing the communal or the Christian card, they could easily win over the loyalties of the majority of prominent Kerala Congress leaders from the Central Travancore area. The only exception was late T. M. Jacob who initially remained elusive on the question of replacing K. Karunakaran from the CM's post. But ultimately Jacob too was placated to the camp of anti-Karunakaran forces through shrewd moves at the instance of certain church leaders.

However, the stand of the league party was crucial. Their shrewd leaders wanted to make maximum political mileage during this serious crisis in the ruling alliance. The venue of the political battle had shifted from the state capital to their citadel in northern Kerala. The traditional house of league supremo became alive. Mr Clean in Congress party operating from behind the curtain and guiding his loyalist protégé in the revolt against the leader made a couple of trips to the supremo's house during January 1995, obviously to read his mind on this issue. But he remained evasive as if he is least interested in the group politics in Congress. Led by the Congress' party's then Chanakya in Tamil Nadu and propped up by senior intelligence sleuths, clandestine counter-moves were made to retain the support of the league for the beleaguered leader. Through intermediaries, they too established contact with the supremo.

The inside story in the league shared by one of its senior most functionaries—aristocratic, highly secular and affable—was that the party was yet to reach a consensus on Karunakaran's issue. Many senior leaders felt that it is not a wise political move to go against Karunakaran, who was always keener to safeguard the interests of the party in alliance politics. Their concern was more on his successor. To them, Mr Clean who was strongly propped up by the faction opposed to Karunakaran was not a match for the leader, as he can never rise up to latter's mass appeal. They had genuine doubts on his potential to lead their front to victory in the next assembly polls in 1996. But the detractors of this line, notably the party's senior minister in the cabinet, made a shrewd move to the effect that they are not against the leader but his style of functioning, particularly his adamant stand of shielding a senior police officer, not acceptable to their community. Ironically, both the camps could not precisely read the mind of the party supremo; nor the warring Congress factions. Obviously, the move of Mr Narasimha Rao was to ascertain the stand of the league party on this vexed issue.

My mind full of such past images and thoughts, I reached the traditional house of the supremo on the next day early morning. The spacious camp office adjacent to the house, normally crowded by followers or those seeking alms and blessings from the supremo, who is also the spiritual head of the community, had a deserted look. With sleepy eyes, the old fragile attendant of the house rushed to me and left with a meaningful smile. Actually, he served the supremo as his personal secretary and managed all kinds of visitors. Over the years, he had become friendly to me by virtue of my occasional visit to the place.

I didn't wait long; the supremo himself opened the door with his unique smile. Instead of the spacious reception hall where he usually met the visitors, he directed me to a small study room adjacent to the bedroom.

'I think that you have some urgent mission; that is why you took the trouble to meet me too early this morning', he asked me to get seated.

'Thank you Sahib, you have rightly sensed the purpose of my mission.' With a pleasing smile, I explained the whole mission. He had a patient hearing and then responded:

'Normally, our party takes decision on all such important issues in our high power committee; I will announce it in the larger party forum or through a press meet. As regards to the change of leader of the ruling front, discussions are on to finalize our stand. But I wonder whether the leader was involved in all such scandals and controversies that appear in the newspapers.'

He paused for a moment. His *Beebee*[22] came in with two cups of steaming black coffee and disappeared into the bedroom.

....
[22] This colloquial word means wife or better half.

Sipping the black coffee, I pointed out:

'Such doubts are there at all levels from the level of PM to the common people in the streets. Naturally, the purpose of the proposed meeting of the PM with you is to discuss such political issues connected with the controversy. As it is exclusively a private affair, you as the head of the party can share your thoughts and impressions with him.'

I tried to clarify the position in line with our mission.

'Then what should I say about the entire controversy, especially the demand for the removal of the leader? Already, the senior Congress leaders from both the groups have met me and explained their line. I patiently listened to their arguments, but didn't comment about my stand. In such a scenario, even if I go to Delhi, I will be unable to spell out anything on the matter unless and until the party takes a final decision.'

His query has naturally put me in a dilemma, I tried to wriggle out of the situation.

'As far as I know, the removal of the CM is one among the many issues perhaps the PM is interested in; there are other interrelated issues such as the political fallout of the decision, communal repercussions, the future of the ruling front, etc. And definitely, you can interact with party leaders and assess their stand before proceeding to Delhi within a couple of days, for which travel arrangements will be made from our side, without coming to open.'

I explained the mission in a lighter tone, creating an impression that the head of the nation is interested to have a personal meeting with the most popular religious leader in Kerala, who played a decisive role in maintaining peace and harmony in Kerala in the aftermath of the demolition of the Babri Masjid.

The inherent weakness of any human being to succumb to the temptations of ego and self-pride had influenced the psyche of the party supremo, who half-heartedly agreed to the proposal and gave the green signal to work out the formalities. Back to office, I was eager to convey the good news to the state chief, but his landline remained engaged.

While waiting impatiently to establish contact with the boss, abruptly my office telephone rang. From the other side, I heard the coarse unfamiliar sound.

'Hi, Richard, don't play with fire. I am the state minister. You have no business to arrange a visit of our party chief to New Delhi and make him issue some statements to embarrass our party. Who asked you to do this dirty trick? If you go ahead with this game, tomorrow the whole world will come to know about the role of your organization. I know nobody can defend you.'

He was really in a furious mood.

'Sir, you have misunderstood the entire thing. I only discussed about his personal views on the present ISRO controversy with a suggestion that New Delhi is keen to know the line of approach of ruling front parties on the ongoing demand to remove the CM. Even the PM is ready to give personal audience to those leaders intended to meet him in Delhi.'

I tried to wriggle out of the situation.

'Don't try to get out of the mess. I know everything about your moves. Better never than late, end your dirty game.' He abruptly stopped the talk; I felt that he was still furious.

I was plunged into utter confusion. The most worrying aspect was that the minister has already come to know about this sensitive operation. Who should have shared this information with the minister? I couldn't make any guess. Other serious concerns agitated my mind: Whether the enraged minister would make the issue public to garner support for his line against the leader? How will I convince my boss about the failure of the mission?

While I was in the whirlpool of such worried thoughts, the telephone rang again. With a thudding heart, I lifted the receiver. From the other side, I heard his feeble sound.

'Hope that you have met him and worked out the details?' It was the state chief.

I explained the entire episode and the veiled threat of the minister. There was absolute silence on the other end; that had really surprised me. But I was really taken aback when he abruptly started to respond.

'How did the minister come into the picture; I told you to discuss the matter only with your "friend". Is this the way you handle a sensitive operation? Don't go ahead with the task; if any adverse falls out, you face the music. I have to cut a sorry face before the chief in Delhi.'

I was sure that he was really annoyed, but I sincerely desired to clear my stand.

'Sir, as you are aware, "our friend" discussed such crucial issues with the concerned minister.' I tried to set right my position.

'That is all right, but how the name of our organization is brought into the matter? That is my real concern; you should have properly briefed him to keep the entire matter secret.' He stuck to his line putting the entire blame on me.

Logic or practical wisdom seldom had had any impact in arriving at such self-centred conclusions and convictions which are the hallmark of the majority of our senior bosses. Success in any highly difficult sensitive assignments or operations would be treated as feathers in their cap, whereas failures in such missions are attributed as lack of professionalism or lack of commitment of the ground level operatives. Such a culture has become an anathema to motivation and true professionalism of a number of ground level operatives in our security and investigation organizations. Thus, the attitude of the local boss didn't surprise me.

The worrisome thought was how the minister would play up the issue in his political checkerboard to win the game of unseating the veteran leader. Abruptly, what struck my mind was the image of that affable and affluent leader of the league party with whom I had cordial relations.

When I reached his aristocratic bungalow situated on a small hillock on the suburbs of the busy business township, he was enjoying the fasting month of Ramadan in the midst of his grandchildren on vacation. Soon, the grandchildren disappeared to the sprawling lawns behind the house.

'I know the reason for your hasty visit. Both the party supremo and the minister discussed the issue in detail. The party chief, as you know, is helpless; he was in fact keen to meet the VVIP in Delhi; but the young minister has different agenda. He wants to emerge as the kingmaker of the new CM after removing the controversial leader. That is why, he was agitated over your secret mission.'

He started with an innocent smile.

His words had soothing effect on my worried mind; the real second in command in league party, a colourful personality with great political legacy knows the facts in right perspective. I felt that there is no need to narrate the entire episode to him.

'Hajee Sahib, you know everything well in advance. As you rightly indicated, our minister is a little bit agitated over the issue. As you know well, sometimes we have to play such games in which we have no control. My only request is that the matter should not be flabbergasted to cause embarrassment to us.'

I sincerely desired to bury the issue forever.

'That you need not worry. I will take care of it, today itself I will talk to him and settle the issue for ever.' Just like an affectionate father, he reassured me with an innocent smile.

Almost after two decades, when I recollect that episode, his image comes across my mind with many emotional memories and episodes. Now no more present with us, he was a politician of the rarest rare breed—highly secular, learned, aristocratic, humane and affable—with a mind to help the needy and poor by spending his own wealth and money. His aristocracy or affluence has never come in the way of helping people from all hues of life. That was the greatness of this leader.

Once the league party had decided to solidly ally with the detractors of the leader in Congress party, the latter's moves to tide over the political tornado that had arisen out of the ISRO scandal had virtually failed. Moreover, aggrieved over the abrupt ascendency of his progeny in the state's political horizon, many of his protégés who held senior positions in the party organization became less vocal in defending the leader.

Thus, at the end of the rancorous group war, 'leader's repeated pleas to the party high command to let him complete his five-year term were turned down, as it became clear that he no longer enjoyed the support of the party's coalition partners'.

Mr A. K. Antony who had only then resigned as Union Civil Supplies Minister on the ground of false aspersions cast on his Ministry in a sugar scandal 'was flown down to Trivandrum on a special aircraft owned by the Indian army to be sworn in as CM'.[23]

Perhaps the Chanakya from Tamil Nadu was the lone voice in the party high command, who defended the leader during this crisis period.

The political storm unleashed by ISRO case that uprooted the veteran Congress leader had, to a great extent, influenced the direction of the Kerala politics. The league party, as envisaged by its leaders, virtually played the role of kingmaker in the front headed by the Congress, thereby immensely improving their stake in the state politics. The party had virtually adopted Mr Clean by offering its traditional citadel of Tirurangadi Assembly constituency in Malappuram district in the crucial by-elections held during 1995. Though he had won the seat by the mercy of the league, Mr Clean, as anticipated by many within Congress and outside, could not

....

[23] M. G. Radhakrishnan, '17 Years On, ISRO Spy Case Comes Back to Haunt AK Antony', *India Today* (2012, 24 October).

demonstrate the political acumen and calibre of his predecessor as the CM.

Meanwhile, the LDF, especially the CPM, as the main opposition resorted to their orchestrated campaign to the effect that the Congress has hushed up the case because it threatened to implicate PM Narasimha Rao's son. The reopening of the case has figured prominently in its election manifesto for 1996 Assembly polls. Riddled with factionalism and personality clashes, the Congress was unable to effectively counter such campaigns. Thus, the United Democratic Front (UDF) suffered a humiliating defeat in 1996 Assembly polls. In June 1996, the new CPM-led LDF government withdrew the consent given to the CBI to probe the case and decided on a reinvestigation of ISRO espionage case by the state police in 1995.

But the storm of ISRO scandal has caused the maximum damage to the state Congress, shaking its foundation of unity and cohesiveness. Whenever the issue openly surfaces, the leaders of different factions use it as a weapon to justify their position or to embarrass the others, directly or indirectly, connected with the controversy. Such trends had become more ominous after the SC verdict in April 1998, exonerating all accused in the case. K. Karunakaran, the worst political victim of the controversy, who held that the verdict had vindicated his stand added, 'if the state government was not ready to repent, the only way out of it was to resign, but I don't demand it'.[24] But the sarcastic response of E. K. Nayanar, the then CPM CM, had virtually embarrassed the Congress leaders: 'Antony and Vayalar Ravi should decide among themselves as who should give compensation for ousting Karunakaran from his *gaddi*. If Antony feels that it was wrong of him to take over as CM after toppling Karunakaran, he should do penance.'[25] However,

....

[24] *The New Indian Express*, 'Political Double Speak as SC Closes Spy Case', *The New Indian Express* (1998, 1 May: 1–9). Cochin.
[25] Nambi Narayanan, 'No Need for Apology on ISRO Case', *The Indian Express* (1998, 2 May). Trivandrum.

A. K. Antony as opposition leader in the state maintained that the judgement exposed the vindictive stand of the LDF government, which had ordered the reinvestigation in order to justify its earlier political stand.

Mr Clean and his loyalists tried to absolve themselves from the sin of ousting the octogenarian leader from the CM's post by linking to ISRO case, but the hard truth was that they played the crucial role in this operation. Neither the whole water of River Periyar nor the scents of Arabia can clean their hands. Their occasional confessions or frustrated outbursts on the issue are the clear expressions of their guilty conscience. Cherian Philip, a close aide of Mr Clean, who had led the battle against Karunakaran, had subsequently disclosed that an operational room was opened in the house of one of their loyalist leaders in the heart of the state capital. The key players of the operation were directly or indirectly in touch with sections of sleuths and investigators to get the inside story of the interrogation/investigation, day in and out. Such inputs were conveniently used or misused to target the leader. A set of pliable journalists worked day and night to sensationalize and disseminate such misinformation through the print and digital media. Ironically, this disinformation campaign influenced not only the leaders of almost all major political parties but also sections of bureaucracy and even the judiciary!

But truth cannot be covered or twisted for long; the details of the 'Operation Ouster' have started surfacing after a span of over two decades. Cherian Philip, presently a Marxist fellow traveller, through a Facebook post coinciding with fifth death anniversary of the leader in 2015, said:

> Today is 'leader' Karunakaran's fifth death anniversary. I am publicly apologising for being a partial participant in the heinous act which toppled him from the post of Chief Minister. I am doing this now as the sense of guilt is haunting me even after 20 years.[26]

....

[26] V. R. Jayaraj, 'Ex-Cong Leader Apologises for Toppling Karunakaran Govt in ISRO Spy Case', *The Pioneer* (2015, 24 December). Kochi.

He added:

> During 1994–95, the 'A' group in the Congress, headed by Antony and Chandy, had tarnished Karunakaran's image by describing him as a spy and nation's enemy, Cherian said in the FB post. 'Those who had submitted a chargesheet against him to the high command and held public meetings all over the State demanding his resignation should feel remorse at least at this stage.[27]

However, Mr Clean's loyalists continue to bat on his favour. Twisting history, Oommen Chandy, the former CM during February 2016, came out with an argument that 'neither he nor Antony had demanded the resignation of K. Karunakaran in 1995 based on ISRO Spy case; the resignation was due to difference of opinion in the Rajya Sabha candidate selection!'[28] Besides Oommen Chandy, other senior leaders like P. J. Kurien, former Rajya Sabha vice chairman, Vayalar Ravi and Mullappally Ramachandran (both former Union minsters), M. M. Hassan (president, Kerala Pradesh Congress Committee [KPCC]), etc., were keener to bail out Mr Clean from the controversy. However, they were critical of the manner in which the leader was unceremoniously ousted from the CM's post in 1995.

While his protégés, who enjoyed many privileges within the party and outside, deserted the leader during the most crucial phase of his political career, the stand of his siblings in the party hierarchy, especially K. Muraleedharan and Ms Padmaja Venugopal, was considerably influenced by the developments in the party. Quite naturally, in the wake of the SC verdict, they raised a demand for a probe into the political conspiracy behind the case and action against the three officers in Kerala Police whom the CBI found in 1996 to have fabricated the espionage scandal. They were highly sceptical of the decision of the UDF ministry headed by Oommen

---

[27] Ibid.
[28] G. Rajiv, 'Karunakaran Did Not Resign on ISRO Spy Case: Oommen Chandy', *The Times of India* (2016, 3 February).

Chandy to close the file warranting action against the three police officials involved in the case. Their main target was Chandy who, according to many, had led the campaign against Karunakaran, linking ISRO scandal, whereas they accused Ramesh Chennithala, one-time close loyalist of the leader of doing nothing to redeem Karunakaran's name.

But once Muraleedharan, who was on political wilderness for long, was re-inducted into the party, he had softened his stand on the entire controversy. Though fully aggrieved over the ignominious removal of his father from CM's post, branding him as traitor and anti-national, he has been now sermonizing the rank and file of the party to forget the past for ever for the larger sake of the unity and cohesiveness of the party! Thus, in 2012, he found a way out to exonerate the state Congress leaders from the controversy attributing that former PM P. V. Narasimha Rao who had asked the leader to resign had a hand in the political conspiracy.[29] Moreover, he found that Rao's goal was to finish off the career of all senior Congress leaders who he thought had the potential to become PM!

But the hard truth was that Rao had never betrayed the leader, but explored all efforts to douse the fire within the party and to retain him as the CM. But when he was convinced that the ruling alliance in Kerala is at the brim of a split and the Congress MPs from the state are gradually turning against him, he had no other alternative but to disown the leader. That was a shrewd political move of Rao to save his chair and the party in Kerala. The hard reality is that politics and political ambitions are thicker than friendly or blood relations!

....

[29] *The Hindu*, 'Narasimha Rao's Name Dragged into ISRO Spy Case', *The Hindu* (2012, 3 October). Trivandrum.

GAME OVER: CBI VERSUS IB   13

During the second week of February 1995, when I received an urgent call from our state headquarters, I was really surprised. There was one-line instruction: to reach there on the next day.

The next day, on reaching the headquarters, I went straight to the room of the ISRO case nodal officer—the tiny, timid officer with tired heart. In the overcrowded room, I saw familiar gloomy faces—interrogators, tech people, secret enquiry and surveillance experts—all those associated with ISRO espionage case.

Soon, we were led to the chamber of the chief, who too had a beleaguered look. In a choked voice, he welcomed us.

'You will be surprised why you were summoned on a short notice. Over the last couple of months, we all meticulously worked to unearth the espionage network targeting our space establishments. Whatever inputs that we gathered through interrogation and other channels were shared with CBI and other investigation agencies. But, to our utter surprise and concern, the CBI had come out with their findings that no evidence on espionage could be unearthed and that many of our inputs based on interrogation of the suspects are found to be incorrect. Thus, we have to critically examine the CBI findings. For that purpose, you may go through the IRs and specifically cite the incriminating facts indicating the commission of offense or malpractice along with your comments on the glaring bottlenecks on the CBI findings. You complete the task on war footing as we have to send a consolidated feedback to Delhi.'

The local chief concluded his words. We soon retreated to the room of the nodal officer and started the exercise. Going through the reference report of the CBI, I was convinced that they had undertaken detailed investigation into various incriminating facts connected with case or the key players of the espionage story. Thus, the crucial question was how we can demolish such findings by using the disclosures of the accused—sometimes truth, semi-truth or always total lies.

In fact, the CBI came up with the stunning conclusion that the key meetings and transactions that were said to have been proof that the spy ring existed had never taken place. The key persons mentioned in the meeting were not present in those places.

One such crucial meeting was that held at Madras International Hotel on 24 January 1994 in which all the key players of the spy network attended, and transaction of money and documents had taken place. The CBI furnished unflinching evidence to substantiate that no such meeting took place there. First, no reservation was made in the hotel in the name of any of the persons as claimed by the investigators. Zuhaira, the key figure of the meeting, as per Interpol's report, had only one valid passport and did not travel to India in 1994; Dr Sasikumaran had attended a funeral of his mother-in-law (Smt Janaki) in Quilon, Kerala, on 24 January and could not be present at the hotel; IG Srivastava was present in Trivandrum on that day as showed from wireless records, his personal car (No. KL02A 9100) log and statements made by Shri V. R. Rajeevan, the then commissioner of police, Trivandrum, and Chandrasekaran's visit to Madras was on 18 June and not on 24 June as confirmed by the statements of his close relatives.

Another meeting of the similar nature was the one that was held in Hotel Luciya, Trivandrum, on 23 September 1994, when the accused ISRO scientists had received a stupendous sum of US$0.9 million from Zuhaira for exchanging vital documents and drawings of Vikas Engine. Just like the Madras meeting, CBI established that this meeting too had come out of the imagination of the accused or the interrogators/investigators. Zuhaira, as confirmed by CBI, didn't visit India in 1994; both the accused ISRO scientists attended office on the aforementioned date as testified by three senior scientists of ISRO and above all the Room No. 108 in which the secret meeting was claimed to be held was occupied by Naikwadi, Air India Officer, transferred from Bombay to Trivandrum.

Similarly, CBI demolished reports on the meetings reported to have been held in Hotel Fort Manor, Trivandrum, in 1990 and during March and June 1994. The fact that the Hotel Fort Manor became operational only on 21 December 1991 has further exposed the inconsistencies and falsies in the interrogation statements and police investigations!

The CBI has established that Maldivian ladies along with other key players of the spy ring didn't visit Indiranagar Club, Bangalore, in September 1994, as claimed by investigators. In the case of Nambi Narayanan, CBI found that he had never met either Mariam or Fauzia. Both the ladies failed to identify Raman Srivastava in pictures or in real life.

On the basis of detailed probe into the background, activities and financial status of the key players of the case, CBI brought out entirely different personal profiles of those players, as against those compiled by initial investigators. Contrary to the image that Nambi Narayanan was affluent and leading a luxurious life, CBI presented a different picture, highlighting that 'anyone making money illegally is unlikely to have just one, 14-inch black and white television set in the house'. The CBI *panchnama* (inventory) of properties recovered from his house mainly consisted of insignificant items such as six cane chairs, two tables, a couple of lamps and so on. He had even sold his car and refrigerator to meet financial exigencies. Suspicions that he had bought property elsewhere proved false. He had only advised a friend in Trivandrum to set up an aquaculture farm and hoped to work with him after retirement. His son had taken up a ₹2,500 per month job.

In the case of Sasikumaran, the CBI found no proof of his involvement in espionage. However, CBI did not make detailed probe into his assets which, according to the police investigators, included blue-chip share certificates, title deeds, two buildings in Trivandrum city and 1.5 acres of land in an industrial estate in Tamil Nadu. One contention from CBI circles, in this regard, was that they were investigating offences under Official Secrets Act and not under the Prevention of Corruption Act. CBI claimed that the systematic questioning of the accused and the verification of documents have confirmed that he has procured these assets not out of any illegal money. Similarly, he could properly explain the circumstances and reasons for the possession of drawings and photocopy of documents related to the Vikas Engine and the GSLV technology, recovered from his residence, by investigation agencies. CBI also established his contacts with Maldivian ladies, but could not establish the claim of investigators that he had taken one of them (Fauzia) to the ISRO complex where she took photographs. The CBI says she, instead, went for picnic to the Aruvikkara Dam site, a common tourist spot near Trivandrum, along with several other Maldivians who have been interrogated and ascertained the truth.

Though initial reports presented Mariam as a yet another Mata Hari and the pivot of the espionage plot, the CBI report confirmed her as a lower level functionary of the Maldivian Secret Service, assigned with the task of monitoring those Maldivians in India, suspected of plotting a coup against President Abdul Gayoom. She was not like a Bond girl living in luxuries, but lived virtually in penury, staying in cheap hotels, eating in third-class restaurants and travelling in the cheapest modes of transport. Yet she had the propensity to make friends at airports or hotels and end up with them in their houses or other places of entertainment!

CBI report mentions that this mercurial capacity led Ahmed Fouad Jizawi, chairman of the Riyadh-based Al Foadia General Trading and Contracting Company, to pick her up from Trivandrum Airport and when she finally ended up in Kovalam Beach Resort, the only time she stayed in a fancy hotel. Jizawi paid her bills, and she spent most of her time in his room. CBI which probed into this meeting with the help of Interpol reached the conclusion that this was no more than a casual tryst and Jizawi was an ordinary trader and not an arms merchant, as scripted by the interrogators. CBI claimed that the contacts of Mariam and Fauzia with Chadrasekharan and Sasi were of such nature.

CBI found that Chandrasekharan, as representative of GK, was hands in glove with the key functionaries of the Russian company. As liaison man, he maintained excellent rapport with many senior officials of ISRO and had done everything to keep them in good humour. His prime concern was to ensure the receipt of commission and other perks from GK and allied establishments dealing with ISRO. In this connection, two bank transactions involving Chandrasekharan had attracted the attention of CBI. First, he had transferred an amount of \$4,500 (₹1.41 lakh) from the State Bank of India branch in New York to the account of a company called Technomash in Republic National Bank of New York. Second, an amount of \$15,000 (₹4.5 lakh) had been transferred by a Russian company to Chandrasekharan's account in Hong Kong and Shanghai Bank in Singapore. Naturally, there would be genuine doubts that these payments could be for dubious activities like espionage. But these curious transactions were meant to evade Indian taxes with his employers making payments in foreign accounts. At the same time, GK maintained an escrow account (No CS 002) in Bangalore branch of the Bank of Rajasthan opened in March 1992 and operated under the signature of Professor A, chairman of GK.

Alexi Vasin of GK, who was in touch with ISRO officials as early as in 1985, figured prominently in the case for his suspected involvement in corporate espionage. As per the initial IRs of different agencies, he with the help of the accused ISRO scientists was involved in transferring the drawings and technology of Vikas Engine to a number of countries including Brazil, Pakistan, Malaysia and North Korea. According to the CBI report, Vasin was questioned by the Russia's Economic Crime Department of the Federal Counterintelligence Services and he denied the charges, saying there was no need to buy drawings of an engine more than 20 years old when his own country had made far more powerful ones. Professor Duyenv had also reiterated the earlier line by holding: 'those who are initiating such inquiries did not obviously have any technical expertise, let alone any idea of rich legacy of India–Russia space cooperation'.

Ironically, some other players who had surfaced during the interrogation of the accused, according to CBI, could not be traced or linked to the espionage story. One such character, who was created with the image of a Bond girl, was Zuhaira. The Interpol report revealed that Zuhaira Omar (born in 1948), a Malé national (Address: Cananige, Galolu) and related to Fauzia has been temporarily staying in Colombo (No. 3, Charlie Mount Road) for business purpose. She was married to Abdullah Mohammed in 1977 and got one son and one daughter. Apart from business trips to India, the Interpol could not cater any input linking her espionage activities.

As revealed by the interrogation statements, Mazar Khan, a senior officer in the Pakistan High Commission (PHC) at Colombo, was another character. To establish Khan's identity, the CBI requested the cabinet secretariat to send photographs of the personnel employed at the PHC. The cabinet secretariat forwarded 14 photographs of some members of the PHC in Colombo, with their names indicated behind the photographs. However, none of the accused was able to identify Khan.

Mohiyuddin, assistant manager of Habib Bank in Malé, has also figured in IRs. The inquiries conducted by CBI through the Interpol in Malé and Sri Lanka showed that no person by the name of Mohiyuddin worked in the Habib Bank in Malé. This bank, as claimed by Indian intelligence agencies, is a front for ISI's (Inter-Services Intelligence of Pakistan) financial transactions in South Asia. Incidentally, Fauzia Hassan was an ex-employee of the Habib Bank, Malé. The CBI held that same was the case of Mehboob Pasha, a Pakistani businessman based in Colombo whose name had surfaced for his alleged links with ISI.

By making a detailed probe into the functioning and operations of ISRO, the CBI contradicted many claims made by other agencies. In this regard, the CBI report referred an internal security audit of documents conducted at the instance of the chairman, ISRO. As per the report, no document was missing in the cryo area, but in the non-cryo area, 254 documents of a random nature were found missing. Moreover, the ISRO authorities vouched that it follows an open door policy in regard to issuing documents to scientists and, as in any research organization, scientists are free to study documents in the documentation cell or library and copies of these documents can also be issued to various divisions on an indenting procedure. CBI claimed that interrogation of senior scientists revealed that it was usual for scientists to take documents/drawings home for discussions or study. They reiterated their stand that mere procurement of drawings or documents would not lead to actual transfer of technology for which the involvement of human resources is inevitable.

One of the serious disclosures that had sensationalized the espionage story was the dubious linkages of the Hyderabad-based businessman Ravindra Reddy's company MTAR. Reddy is said to be related to Vijaya Bhaskara Reddy, former CM of Andhra Pradesh, and allegedly had business dealings with Prabhakar Rao, son of former PM P. V. Narasimha Rao. In fact, technology transfer outside ISRO was an established practice for many decades. MTAR, Godrej, Larsen & Toubro (L&T) and Walchandnagar Industries, Mumbai, were major players in the fabrication and supplying components to ISRO. Naturally, these firms were in possession of drawings/designs of the vital components of cryogenic and Vikas Engines.

Thus, CBI has made a detailed probe on this issue and it was established that the contract for manufacture of three Vikas Engines was signed on 15 September 1989 when it was formally cleared by the contract negotiation committee consisting of the director, LPSC, and the additional secretary, defence. The report claimed that there was no evidence or proof linking MTAR with the so-called espionage network or their alleged moves to sell the technology to any foreign country. As part of investigation, Ravindra Reddy and others connected with the firm were questioned by the agency.

The Ural Aviation, a Russian air cargo company, was allegedly involved in airlifting tonnes of secret documents of ISRO for transferring to foreign countries interested in space technology. A key disclosure was that with the busting of the spy ring, a package was still lying uncollected in the Moscow Air Cargo. The CBI liaised with the Airports Authority of India (AAI) and confirmed the existence of three Ural Aviation flights in 1994 (URL-224 from Karachi landed Trivandrum on 23 January 1994 and departed for Sharjah on 25 January 1994; URL-9001 from Ras Al khaimah landed on 11 March 1994 and left for Ras Al Khaimah on 13 March 1994 and URL-3791 landed on 17 July 1994 and left for Mumbai on 20 July 1994). A request to verify whether any consignment was lying at the airport was sent to the Indian embassy at Moscow through the Ministry of External Affairs and the reply was: 'Even the international airport has several cargo storage places and it is impossible to make an inquiry on the basis of available information.' In fact, Ural had a contract for airlifting satellite components from ISRO to Moscow and vice versa. Their contract with ISRO for carrying consignments from USSR went into trouble when Indo-USSR Space Agreement was abruptly snapped in December 1993.

Once this exercise of perusing the CBI refer report and interrogation statements of the suspects was over, we reassembled to find out the grey areas or the bottlenecks in CBI findings. Those who were haunted by the evil spirit of espionage and not prepared to reconcile with their professional blunders have come out with a number of fancied claims and arguments to contradict CBI stand on various issues. They vehemently argued that CBI instead of unravelling the espionage network tried to hush up the entire case through hazardous and superficial investigations. The CBI's attempts at investigations abroad, according to them, were far from satisfactory. Thus, the exact role played by key characters like

Alexi Vasin, Zuhaira, Mohiyuddin, Mazar Khan, Mehboob Pasha, etc., could not be unearthed.

They blamed CBI for not making serious efforts to push Interpol for more extensive inquiries about these suspects who probably might have operated in pseudonyms. Had the external intelligence agency been associated with such investigations, a different picture would have emerged, they argued. The CBI team instead of conducting a personal inquiry/physical verification to confirm the presence of consignment of documents airlifted by Ural Aviation in the cargo area of Moscow Airport had taken for granted the superficial reply by the Ministry of External Affairs. Similarly, the CBI had given much sacrosanct to the so-called audit of ISRO's documents, despite the fact that the accused had made categorical statements that only photocopies of the drawings were transferred.

The senior bosses were trigger happy in unearthing these gross bottlenecks in CBI investigations and decided to take up the matter with higher formations in New Delhi to reopen the investigation of the case. But I felt that the CBI would not submit a hotchpotch report on a sensational espionage case, as it would be subjected to thorough judicial scrutiny. On the contrary, secret agencies enjoying the immunity of their reports or findings from open judicial scrutiny very often make compromises on matters of legality or objectivity in the name of secrecy.

Thus, logic said that challenging the CBI findings on flimsy grounds would only strain the relations between two premier agencies dealing with national security. Moreover, except the interrogation statements of the accused—distorted and concocted stories full of lies and contradictions—there was nothing specific or concrete to establish an espionage case in the entire operations. Even the enquiry reports from the fields indicated that more than 90 per cent of the disclosures made by the accused during interrogation were nothing but figments of imagination or well-woven stories. Further, none of the established tradecraft tools, normally used to unearth espionage cases, was followed. Instead of quietly putting suspects under surveillance, tapping their phones, uncovering contacts and setting up sting operations, they were hastily arrested and subjected to marathon interrogation. The final question that came to my mind was what professional or moral right we have to challenge the findings of CBI arrived at through systematic investigation?

There was no coordination between the various agencies either at the ground level or at the level of their top brass. Instead, they tried to establish credibility to their half-baked reports or the old inputs generated by their unprofessional personnel for their survival. Thus, the external intelligence agency, while reincarnating a whole lot of names of agents and subagents deeply involved in the case and operating from Malé, Colombo, Islamabad and Moscow, could not cater any worthwhile inputs establishing their linkages or espionage activities. Instead, many of their officials were in the forefront of turf-battles and blame games particularly targeting the CBI. Same was the case with other agencies including the SIT of the police, which instead of seriously working on the task of collecting evidence adhering to the due process of law religiously followed the uncorroborated and illogical findings of the other agencies. Thus, influenced by the public rhetoric, senior scientists of ISRO were arrested without any iota of evidence or sticking on the basic canons of law and procedures.

Ironically, in such a hectic race to grab credit and accolades, everyone associated with the case from top to bottom jumped into hasty conclusions without properly verifying the veracity of the disclosures or checking the venires and dates of crucial meetings among the alleged plotters. Perhaps, the best example is a classified CBI report which states: 'The Director IB (DIB) sent several notes to important functionaries little realising that these notes from the DIB would be treated as authentic and having been sent after careful verification and consequences of report being false or untrue would be serious.'[30] The same report refers

---

[30] B. R. Srikant, Rajesh Joshi and Venu Menon, 'ISRO Case—IB Imagined Spy-Ring: CBI', *Outlook* (1998, 18 May).

about an 'Unofficial Note (No. 303/DESP/94) on November 21, 1994 saying that a Hyderabad-based businessman, MTAR Ravindra Reddy, an important person in the spy-ring had "business dealings" with Prabhakar Rao, son of the then Prime Minister P. V. Narasimha Rao'.[31] The crucial question arises why such sensational disclosures without any ground level inquiries or verification were leisurely communicated to the highest political executive of the country and whole lot of key functionaries giving ample scope to the media and others to build up sensational stories bringing discredit and causing unprecedented damage to the image of the political head and the government in power? In fact, such unfortunate happenings connected with the ISRO espionage case led to the ignominious downfall of a veteran Congress leader in Kerala and his party's electoral debacle in the subsequent state assembly elections.

....
[31] Ibid.

THE GHOST THAT HAUNTED IB

14

With the submission of CBI's refer report, bad news started pouring in against those interrogators and initial investigators of the ISRO espionage case. The first target, no doubt, was the then DIB, who was indicted for mishandling the investigation and sending unverified reports to the PM and home minister.[32] There were also speculations that his exit from the organization during August 1996, just after a tenure of less than two years, was the fallout of ISRO case. The super-sleuth Bengali Dada, the real architect of the ISRO case, who built up castles in the air for extension of his service, was crestfallen when his pending case for change of date of birth in service records was flatly rejected and superannuation papers were abruptly served at his doorstep. The Damocles' sword of repatriation was hanging over the head of three senior IPS officers who were serving the Bureau in Kerala.

In the midst of such apprehensions and fears, I received a call from the state headquarters of the Bureau to immediately report there. I too anticipated some bad news; that proved to be correct on reaching the headquarters. What was waiting for me was a witness notice dated 2 May 1995 issued under the seal and signature of the investigation officer, Special Police Establishment, New Delhi. The notice in Hindi and English was a notice to witness.[33]

[32] Ibid.
[33] Mentioned at the end of the chapter.

What surprised me was the casual nature of the notice with ambiguities on the name and particulars of the addressee. Moreover, not all officers associated with case were issued with such notice. Though more than two dozen officers of various agencies were actively involved in the interrogation of the suspects, why only nine officers of the Bureau were hand-picked to serve with witness notices, besides half a dozen state police officers closely associated with the investigation?

On discussing such discrimination and ambiguities, the state Bureau chief had ready-made answers. He had no role in preparing the list of officers; instead, the CBI investigators prepared the list based on their inquiries. As the instruction from Delhi headquarters was to serve the notices to all concerned, he had to obey the orders and could not keep anything pending on the grounds of ambiguities, etc. His message was clear: I am bound to accept the ambiguous witness notice!

Thus, the next scene was in New Delhi. The three IPS officers landed there well in advance and were accommodated in safe and secure 'safe houses' in the capital. The ordeal of a couple of us was horrendous. We had to travel in unreserved compartments and had tough time to find accommodation in poorly manned trainees' hostels in New Delhi.

Initially, we all assembled at the establishment branch of the Bureau in the capital. From the very beginning, our nodal officer from Kerala Bureau who was closely associated with the case since beginning felt shaky fearing how the CBI officers would deal with him? He was constantly haunted by the filmy images of CBI officers using third-degree methods to extract confession from the accused during questioning. The senior bosses tried to boost up his sagging morale, but in vain.

A couple of senior officers from the headquarters who were directly supervising ISRO espionage case turned up and interacted with us. They tried to create an impression that the entire process was part of a routine exercise by CBI to close the case once for all. Their soothing words that they would take care of the whole issue didn't convince many of us. Some of us raised genuine doubts: why this drama was enacted and how the headquarters officers remained aloof from it? They evaded such queries parroting that they would sort out the issue without adversely affecting the image of the organization. Not fully convinced of their stand, one belligerent officer who refused to cooperate with the exercise was subsequently pacified at the instance of a senior officer in New Delhi. It remained a secret how he pacified him, but whispers were there that he was offered a Police Medal on the occasion of the next Independence Day! When the Kerala chief strongly endorsed the stand of the headquarters, we too had fallen in line with their briefing and decided to appear before the CBI investigators.

The CBI investigator, an officer of the rank of DSP, recorded the statements of the witnesses. The Kerala chief who deposed before him took the stand that his officers had only extended assistance to the state police in the interrogation of the suspects. To the surprise of all of us, he mentioned the names of a few officers who participated in the interrogation, consciously concealing the names of a set of others deeply involved in such exercises. He admitted that the unverified disclosures made by the suspects during interrogation were summarized and communicated to the headquarters with his specific comments. He was not consulted by the headquarters before sending special notes/brief to the higher formations in the government. To a specific question on the video graphing of the interrogation of suspects, he maintained that some officers had secretly videographed the interrogation. To another question, he clarified that he had not given any instruction to anyone to identify and confirm the photograph of the then IGP Raman Srivastava through the arrested Maldivian ladies.

Another IPS officer posted in Mumbai who conducted initial interrogation of Mariam Rasheeda immediately after her arrest in Trivandrum stated that his impression was that Maldivian authorities had engaged this lady to find out the activities of Maldivians in the alleged anti-Gayoom plot. He suspected certain linkages of Mariam and her close friends like Fauzia and Zuhaira with Pak elements in Malé and Colombo, but added that the interrogation could not bring out anything specific in this regard.

The third IPS officer defended his case holding that the IB has played only a complimentary role in the case by assisting the state police in the interrogation of the accused. However, there was no formal written request from the state police authorities seeking the services of their personnel for such tasks. He maintained that as he was assigned with other important tasks, he intermittently associated with the interrogation of Mariam Rasheeda only for a couple of days. Moreover, for more than one fortnight in November 1994, he was in Karnataka in connection with VVIP visit duties. On a specific question on the preparation of videotapes on interrogation, he claimed that he was not in a position to comment on their genuineness or otherwise. To another question, he held that he didn't share any input relating to the suspected involvement of IGP Raman Srivastava in the case to the state police investigators. Similarly, while remaining posted as commandant of CISF, VSSC, Thumba from January 1984, he did not submit any report against Nambi Narayanan nor advised Kerala Police against the search of his residence in connection with the espionage case. On the question of transfer of sensitive documents in exchange of US$0.9 million to the key accused of the case during their meeting in Trivandrum during September 1994, he pleaded ignorance.

The bespectacled officer from Delhi—the sole personnel from the headquarters—who was summoned by CBI to record statement joined us with the information that the CBI was inclined to fix responsibility over the Bureau officers for the alleged fabrication of a sensational espionage case involving senior space scientists. His disclosure led to increased heart palpitations of many of us.

The CBI officer who recorded the statements tried to ascertain the role of individual officers during interrogation, whether they used any third-degree methods or videographed the interrogation, extracted false confessions to implicate others in the case, submitted written signed statements or received any specific instructions from higher-ups, etc. The CBI investigator put specific questions as how the name of IGP Srivastava had surfaced during interrogation and the manner how his photograph was identified by the accused persons. He also tried to create an impression that they are all birds of the same feather and official duties compelled him to be formal during the entire proceedings.

Officers, except our nodal officer, successfully withstood the exercise sticking to the claim that they had had no investigative powers, but only assisted the police in interrogation process as directed by their superiors.

The exercise ended on a cordial note; the second in command of the CBI had an informal interaction with the officers in their spacious conference hall. He narrated the long saga of his investigation of sensational cases and cited that occupational hazards are an inevitable element in the career of intelligence and investigation professionals. In respect of the ISRO case, he felt that the unsavoury comments from certain corners against the agency was unwarranted as they are only undertaking the tasks as per the law. He reassured that the agency or its hierarchy would not resort to any witch-hunting of any of the officers and the entire matter would be settled forever. His words were of great solace to all.

The ghost of ISRO espionage, supposed to be exorcised by CBI through the aforementioned ritual, has reappeared with renewed vigour and vendetta to strike those sleuths associated with the case. This reincarnation was through the columns of leading English and regional dailies during 1998.

These reports[34] highlighted that the Union Home Ministry has asked the IB to conduct a departmental enquiry (DE) against nine IB officers against their alleged role in the frame-up in the sensational ISRO espionage case. The IB officers against whom the enquiry would be conducted were Mr Mathew John, joint

---

[34] B. R. Srikant, Rajesh Joshi and Venu Menon, 'ISRO Case—IB Imagined Spy-Ring'.

director, Mr R. B. Sreekumar, Mr C. M. Ravindran, both deputy directors (all IPS officers), Mr C. R. R. Nair, Mr G. S. Nair, Mr K. V. Thomas, Mr John Punnen and Mr V. K. Maini (all deputy central intelligence officers) and Mr Jayaprakash (assistant central intelligence officer). The report further added that the Union Home Minister Mr L. K. Advani had expressed displeasure over the role of IB officials and ordered that departmental charge sheets be served on them. Thus, I was not surprised when I received a Confidential Information Memorandum dated 22 May 2000 from the headquarters enclosing the Ministry of Home Affairs (MHA) Memo No. 1–45022/128/99-Pers-1 dated 19 November 1999. Similar memoranda were received by other eight IB officers, whose statements were recorded by CBI in May 1995. This memorandum pertained to the decision of the Ministry to hold an inquiry against nine IB officers under Rule 14 of Central Civil Services (Classification, Control and Appeal) Rules, 1969. Articles of Charges (10) almost on similar lines along with a statement of the imputation of the misconduct and misbehaviour in support of each article of charge were framed against these officers.

The various charges or allegations as contained in the aforementioned articles inter alia included (a) a few IB officers who were entrusted to investigate into the ISRO espionage case physically took over accused Mariam and some subsequently arrested persons from the lawful custody of Kerala Police without completing legal formalities and conducted independent investigations disassociating the Kerala Police, (b) tortured, ill-treated at least three persons during the investigation, (c) did not prepare written statement of interrogation in respect of two persons and left the IR unsigned in the case of four accused interrogated by them, (d) videographed the interrogation of three accused, but concealed the identity of personnel who had done it, (e) recorded the confession statements of the accused persons but failed to conduct verification of the veracity of the statements, (f) did not share the basis of allegations/inputs collected from the accused in respect of IGP Raman Srivastava with the state police and (g) informed the state police through superior officers (of IB) about the unlikely recovery of documents in the event of search of the house of main accused responsible for bringing secret documents from ISRO installation.

A close scrutiny of the aforementioned Articles of Charges reveals how ignorant and confused are people at higher level on the actual role and functioning of intelligence agencies. Anyone having some basic knowledge about CrPC or criminal investigations may rightly interpret these charges as false, unwarranted and having no basis in law and regulations regarding the functioning of the intelligence organizations.

The IB is not a force or agency constituted under any statute of the legislature. Thus, none of the personnel of IB has any power to investigate into any cases nor they can take cognizance of the offences, register case, collect evidence, arrest persons and question them and indulge in any action in pursuance of such investigations. Nor the IB officials can conduct enquiry verification with the backing of any authority given to them by any regulations. IB cannot force any citizen or institution to part with any information, document or material for that matter however holy may be intentions of the IB in that enquiry.

The crucial question is who had entrusted any investigation to IB? The heart of the matter is that CrPC does not give any power even to MHA to authorize IB to investigate, enquire, probe or even verify anything. If at all any of these activities are done by IB, these are totally clandestine and secret and, therefore, have no legal validity.

If that be the charter of IB or its legal position in respect of investigations and connected procedures, other allegations and imputations would not stand to legal scrutiny. For example, the allegation that the IB personnel physically took over the arrested accused from the lawful custody of police without completing the legal formalities and conducted independent investigations can only be construed as misinterpretation of law and established procedures. The arrested persons throughout the duration of police remand period remain under the physical custody of police.

Moreover, as per the regulations of guarding the arrested persons, according to the provisions of the police manual and other regulations or instructions issued by the higher police formations, police guards are provided to the persons under custody. Besides, for ensuring the security and safety of arrested persons thorough infrastructural physical measures are also taken.

In this background, it would be impossible for anybody to kidnap or whisk away the persons under police custody. Had anybody done so, the accused persons should have complained to police or magistrate to whom they were produced many a time. Nor did the investigation officer or his higher police officers came out with any such allegation or complaint. Same was the case with the allegations of torture or ill treatment of accused during interrogation. Even if there were any such excesses, the legal action can be warranted against the IO of the state police who has the statutory duty to take cognizance of such offence, as this will be the first information report (FIR) revealing the commission of an offense and thereafter register case against the culprits.

The aforementioned statutory standing and legal role of IB in investigation of cases make it clear that they do not have any legal authority or administrative powers for interrogation as part of investigation or enquiry. Thus, preparation of statement of interrogation does not fall under the realm of IB's charter or duties. On the contrary, it is the duty of IO to record such statements under section 162 of the CrPC. Similarly, the question of IB officers recording the confession of the accused is irrelevant. Any such confession by an accused or suspect—though not admissible in the court of law—should be before a police officer, as per Section 25 of the Indian Evidence Act. Moreover, such a task does not fall under the purview of the IB officials who are called by IOs to assist them in the case.

Further, under the provisions of the CrPC, it is the exclusive legal authority or responsibility of the IO of the case to verify each nugget of information forthcoming from the accused during the questioning/interrogation. No officer assisting the IO, particularly when the officer is not belonging to the police force, has the authority to verify the veracity of each point revealed by the accused person during the interrogation or in a perceived confession. Any act of verification of any such facts/points by IB officials would have amounted to interference in the investigation.

In a nutshell, anybody aware of the basic principles of Criminal Justice System and letter and spirit of the CrPC knows that in any investigations, the IO of the case alone has the wholesome authority to initiate any action as part of the investigation. Nobody can intervene or instruct the IOs in such matters. Thus, Lord Denning had rightly observed:

> No minister of the crown can tell him (Investigation Officer) that he must or must not keep observation of this place or that, or that he must or he must not prosecute this man or that, nor can any police authority tell him so. The responsibility for law enforcement lies on him, he is answerable to law and law alone.[35]

In this backdrop, a genuine doubt arises as what exactly is the role of intelligence organizations in such complex issues. The intelligence agencies are the backbone of any country in safeguarding the vital secrets or meeting the challenges that jeopardize the sovereignty, security or integrity of the nation. No doubt, counter-espionage is one of their prime tasks. But there are established mechanisms or strategies to successfully undertake such operations. Any input on any suspected espionage, received from police or sister agencies or generated through HUMINT or TECHINT or other informal channels is developed in utmost secrecy by using a set of intelligence tools (tradecraft mechanisms) such as surveillance of the suspect(s), monitoring of their communication channels, clandestine photography/sting operations, cover assignments/secret enquiry to unearth their activities and network of contacts so as to generate concrete evidence linking their involvement

---

[35] Regina V. Commissioner of Police of the Metropolis Ex-Parte, Blackburn: CA 1968 ([1968] 2 QB 118, [1968] 1 All ER 763, [1968] 2 WLR 893).

in espionage activities. Once such evidence is collected, the police having investigation powers arrest the suspects, subjects them to joint interrogation, confronting them with specific material evidence collected through various clandestine methods. The veracity of their disclosures is further verified through formal investigations for adducing evidence in order to build up a foolproof espionage case for judicial scrutiny/trial and final conviction of the actual culprits.

These issues had come to the fore when the officers of IB against whom departmental inquiry was in the offing met at the Bureau's headquarters in New Delhi during May 2000 in order to work out the future strategy as how the issue could be tackled. A senior officer at the headquarters was designated as coordinating officer to work out the strategy. In fact, all the involved officers were demoralized in one way or other: the Damocles' sword of repatriation had already struck the IPS officers; the cadre officers of the Bureau felt that they had become the scapegoats on believing the words of the CBI investigators. While a couple of them were overanxious about their superannuation papers, others were really concerned about their promotions and deputation assignments including the peacekeeping operations of the United Nations, pending the DE proceedings and vigilance clearance.

These sentiments had echoed during their interaction with the designated officer in his cabin in the North Block. Except the Kerala chief, all others were almost unanimous in their stand not to accept the Articles of Charges legally and factually incorrect with full of contradictions. One of the IPS officers poignant over his repatriation to his parent cadre was highly critical of the approach of the Bureau headquarters, especially the attitude of a couple of officers deeply involved in the case. Though all the officers, now facing the music, acted as per the instructions of these senior officers, neither they took the moral responsibility for the lapses nor were keen to defend the affected officers.

Holding that the Bureau is doing everything to defend the officers, the coordinating officer highlighted the grave omissions and commissions of the state unit in properly handling a suspected espionage case. He was emphatic that it was not the time for witch-hunting or the post-mortem of the past episodes, but to seriously explore legal and other channels to find a way to get out of the present imbroglio. One of the IPS officers pointed out that the Articles of Charges against the officers can be thrown into waste basket by merely quoting the charter of duties of the IB. But the crucial question was whether such a statutory charter that would stand to the legal scrutiny is available or not. None could give a specific or categorical answer to this question.

Finally, an informal meeting with the director was held to discuss such issues and future course of action. He tried to convey a message that he is well aware of the entire episode and would do everything to safeguard the interests of the affected officers and entrusted the coordinating officer to explore legal opinion as how to proceed with the matter. Accordingly, a meeting with an eminent legal luminary from the South and practising in the SC and subsequently elevated as the Solicitor General of India was arranged. The main question raised before the learned attorney was whether the Articles of Charges should be accepted or not. His outright reaction was that once accepted it would become a milestone tied on the neck and would take much time to untie it and free the person from the burden. What were the other options? First, legally challenge the articles of charges. Second, accept the Articles of Charges and cooperate with DE.

The first option, according to the attorney, would lead to a confrontation with the Home Ministry, especially with the CBI. The senior hierarchy of the Bureau, which never ever cherished such a confrontation with Ministry, was always in favour of the second option. The coordinating officer, just like a brilliant negotiator, came out with a more viable option: accept the Articles of Charges and neutralize the future actions at the instance of the senior bureaucrats in the Ministry. His optimism that the Bureau having good clout and rapport with the Home Ministry would be able to settle the matter amicably was well reciprocated by the officers involved. Thus, though half-heartedly, all the nine officers formally accepted the Articles of Charges, much to the relief of the senior bosses.

The defence statement prepared on the basis of the attorney's legal advice and vetted by the coordinating officer was filed by each officer during May 2000, countering the charges and the imputation statements. The main focus of the statement was that the IB being a secret organization not established under any special statute has no legal power for investigations and as such all related allegations and insinuations against the officers in connection with ISRO case have no legal sanctity. The senior bosses' assurance that they would settle matter at the earliest was of much consolation to all. But that consolation was short-lived.

Meanwhile, signals had started emanating from the inner circles of the Bureau that the attempts made by the senior bosses with the Union Home Ministry to drop the charges against the officers could not meet with any success. The intervention of the apex court and the NHRC in the case had virtually panicked the bureaucrats to do anything out of the way. While the SC closed the doors for the reinvestigation of the case, the NHRC recommended an initial compensation of ₹10 lakh to scientist Nambi Narayanan. The courts at various levels were flooded with litigations seeking criminal proceedings against the erred police officers and the enhanced compensation to the victims, etc. It was with great difficulty that the then director managed to defer the in-house probe against the charged officers at the instance of the then Union home minister.[36] However, the minister, under pressure from various corners, especially from a set of senior bureaucrats and sections of scientists, was against exonerating the officers from all charges.

The Kerala government, instead of acting on the spirit of the verdict or directions of the courts or august bodies like NHRC, went out of the way to protect their officers involved in the case.

. . . .

[36] *The Hindu*, 'Advani Orders IB to Defer Probe', *The Hindu* (1998, 7 December: 1).

In fact, following the SC judgement on 29 April 1998, exonerating all the accused in ISRO espionage case, there was dilly-dallying from the part of the successive governments in taking action against the police officials including Siby Mathews, IPS, who headed the SIT.

For more than 13 years, the file proposing action against the erred police officials remained under the carpet, when on 29 June 2011 the then state government headed by the Congress party decided to drop the charges against the officials. The reason ascribed to this decision was that 'it is not proper or legal to take disciplinary action against the officials for the alleged lapses pointed out in the investigation report of the CBI at this juncture, after the lapse of 15 years'. But the most bizarre episode was the appointment of Siby Mathews as chief information commissioner, Kerala, immediately after his voluntary retirement! However, such magnanimity from the part of the state, apparently flouting the legal and statutory norms or principles was not shown to IB's cadre officers!

In the case of the indicted cadre officers of IB, uncertainty and anxiety continued pending the final disposal of the charges framed against them. In New Delhi, new governments had come and gone; Bureau bosses very often made convincing assurances that the charges against all would be dropped. But nothing had happened as promised.

In March 2004, a couple of such cadre officers in IB had become the real scapegoats of the ISRO case. After years of indefinite delay in the case of their promotion to the higher rank due to Bureau's failure to frame promotion rules to that particular cadre, the Departmental Promotion Committee (DPC) had finally met and finalized the list of over 60 officers to be promoted. But three officers associated with the case, but highly eligible for promotion, didn't figure in the list. The DPC had cleared their promotions, but their names were kept in sealed cover pending the completion of DE proceedings. The senior bosses at the headquarters, who time and again assured to protect the career interests of the officers involved in the case, were still hopeful to sort out the issues with the help of bureaucrats. They were not frank enough to admit that all their efforts to get the charges dropped at the instance of the bureaucrats in the Home Ministry failed; nor could they say for certain when and how the DE proceedings would be completed. Strangely, they were also not in favour of the affected victims knocking at doors of judiciary to get justice!

Ultimately, what came to their rescue was the Central Administrative Tribunal (CAT), Kerala, which was moved during June 2004 with the request to issue direction to the DIB, Union Home Secretary and others to grant promotion to these officers. The CAT had to defer its sitting on a couple of times as the respondents failed to file a counter-affidavit. Exasperated over the callous approach, the CAT passed an interim direction to the effect that ex parte decision would be taken in the petition with strictures against the respondents. This had forced the respondents to file a reply statement at a later stage contesting the application.

In the wake of judicial intervention, the Bureau has virtually woken up from its deep slumber. The DE against nine officers which has been pending as early as in 2000 has been reopened. All the officers were urgently summoned to New Delhi during the third week of December 2004. The MHA had appointed a senior IPS officer of the rank of DGP heading a CPMF as inquiring authority. The preliminary hearing was held at his office in New Delhi on 23 December 2004, followed by regular proceedings in Kerala. As eight out of ten charges framed against the officers were dropped by the Government of India, after examining the defence statements, the regular proceedings were conducted in respect of two charges, namely (a) physical custody of accused persons from the lawful custody of Kerala Police without completing legal formalities and conducting independent investigations and (b) torture and ill treatment of at least three persons during the investigation.

Shri R. S. Dhankar, the CBI officer, who was the chief IO of the case and V. R. Rajeevan, IPS, the commissioner of police, Trivandrum, during the relevant period from 22 September 1992 to 29 September 1995 when ISRO case surfaced, had deposed before the inquiry authority. Though Shri D. C. Pathak, the then DIB and Shri Siby Mathews, IPS, the then DIG, SIT, who were issued notices to attend the inquiry proceedings as prosecution witnesses did not attend the proceedings, nor did they send any information to the inquiring authority.

The charged officers produced the order dated 13 January 1995 by the division bench of the Kerala High Court in Writ Appeal No. 1676/94 as defence exhibit to counter the two charges of the physical custody of the accused and their alleged torture and ill treatment. The aforementioned order had categorically asserted that the IB officers had not tortured or ill-treated any of the accused persons during interrogation. As CBI or the Kerala Police had not challenged the order on that issue, the judgement of the division bench of the Kerala High Court can be taken as final. Thus, the inquiring authority after examining the defence exhibits and the statement of witnesses reached the conclusion that there was no evidence to establish the aforementioned charges. Thus, all the nine IB officers were exonerated from the charges framed against them by the MHA on the basis of a special report submitted by the CBI to the Ministry.

But one thing was crystal clear. Had there not been any judicial intervention, there would not have been any DE. It was ironical that it took more than four years to hold the disciplinary enquiry. The MHA/IB, no doubt, had no legal ground to justify this inordinate delay. Thus, instead of contesting the case, they expedited the entire proceedings, dropped all the charges against the officers and filed a statement before the CAT stating that the aggrieved officers, whose promotion had been withheld and kept under sealed cover, were cleared for promotion to the higher rank. Thus, the spirit of judiciary had finally exorcised the ghost of ISRO case that haunted a set of intelligence sleuths for more than one decade!

*

Notice to Witness

(Under section 160Cr. P C S P B-C-VIII

To

(Mr X), Trivandrum, Kerala

(First part in Hindi followed by English version)

Whereas it appears that you are acquainted with the circumstances of the case noted further, which I am now investigating under Chapter XIV of the Code of Criminal Procedure, you are hereby required to attend before me on the 17th day of May 1995 at 10 am at Block No. 3 of CGO Complex, Lodhi Road, New Delhi, for the purpose of answering certain questions relating to the case. Particulars of the case: ₹11 (s)/94-SIU-V/CBI-SIC-II under section 120 (B) of IPC, 3, 4, & 5 of Official Secrets Act (ISRO Espionage case).

Signature, Designation, etc., of Investigating Officer,

Special Police Establishment, New Delhi

Date-2-5-1995

Branch CBI/SIC-II New Delhi

ORCHESTRATED BY AND FOR MEDIA

15

The ISRO spy scandal which virtually came out of the imagination of a mediocre policeman, but cleverly manipulated by a set of political leaders to meet their clandestine agenda, captured the imagination of the people of Kerala at the instance of the vernacular media. Ever since the arrest of the Maldivian ladies, the media recklessly went ahead to weave a sensational espionage story with all ingredients—sex, money and foreign agents.

But their motives were different. A section of them tirelessly tried to increase the circulation of their publications through mere sensationalism. Another group worked day and night to mould up the public opinion in favour of the clandestine political agenda of their mentors. There was yet another lobby which consciously worked to create an impression among the masses that the state is turning into a fuming volcano of anti-national forces backed by hostile neighbours and foreign agents.

The Malayalam media sent correspondents to Maldives and Sri Lanka to dig out the past of these ladies and their key associates. Mariam, Fauzia and Zuhaira were given the dazzling image of Mata Haris with hazy handlers and vast sources of finances. They meticulously tracked what they described as their lascivious romantic life, unearthed their former boyfriends and husbands.

Through series of sensational stories, they unwrapped how they had laid honey trap to ensnare India's top scientists and succeeded in shipping 85 kg of secret documents to Pakistani, Korean and

Dutch interests! Such enchanting media reports had virtually mesmerized Kerala-mind, hungry after such bizarre stories. Their most favourite character, no doubt, was Mariam who figured in headlines as tuna in the bedroom.

Not the ladies alone, but all the suspects and accused had undergone the tragic ordeal of media scanning to dig out details of their personal lives including the horoscope of their kith and kin and printed facts and fiction that suited them. The dividing lines disappeared between tabloids and broadsheets, between rumours and facts, between truth and fiction. For the readers who thought newspaper was the gospel, what they said became the truth. There was no one to question it.

Once the name of Raman Srivastava, IGP, a favourite police officer of the then CM K. Karunakaran, had surfaced in the case, his detractors seized the moment and mounted a campaign against Raman Srivastava. While the opponents of Karunakaran in his party built up an orchestrated campaign to unseat him from CM's chair, the rival political parties in the state used it as a political weapon to tarnish the image of his party and the front. 'Resign Karunakaran' and 'sack Srivastava' became the rallying cry of a frenzied public and the press. By overnight, these parties and their shady leaders became the apostles of internal security, patriotism and nationalism. In such overriding emotions and feelings, the accused and suspects were branded as traitors; they and their lawyers were hounded and pelted with stones wherever they appeared in public.

Even reputed journalists had fallen in the same track of amateurs who created sensational stories out of half-baked leak-outs by police and other agencies. Some among them equated the ISRO spy case as the cleverest cover-up of all time, more than that of Bofors and joined the chorus that the visit of the then PM Narasimha Rao to Trivandrum was part of the cover-up operation by influencing the CBI.

The irony was that nobody questioned the logic of such strange stories planted by the vested interests. Actually, the PM's tour was finalized well in advance in connection with certain programmes in Rajiv Gandhi Centre in Trivandrum. After all what is the need of the PM visiting Trivandrum to suppress the case? If he had any such intentions, he could summon the CBI chief or anybody to Delhi and leave a word of his interest. A few others clamoured that the SC's ruling cannot be the last word in the case, leaving an impression that they are the final judges in such matters!

After the CBI report, there was rethinking among sections of media on their approach towards the espionage case. Such a change of attitude gained further momentum after the SC verdict exonerating all the accused in the case. *India Today* in January 1995 brought out an exclusive investigation story which demolished the espionage theory pointing out around two dozen factual errors or contradictions established by CBI during their investigations. Moreover, by unravelling the earthly realities from the personal lives of Mariam and Fauzia, Shekhar Gupta, the editor of the magazine, to a great extent, could change the Mata Hari image of these ladies, besides throwing more light on the real picture of scientists and others branded as accused/suspects.

The national media played a pivotal role to unfold the real story. *The Hindu, Frontline, Savvy, Sunday Observer*, etc., joined the campaign to bring out the real facts connected with the case. *The Outlook* in May 1998 brought out an exclusive story on ISRO spy case in which they highlighted the classified CBI report that had indicted IB for its unprofessional manner of handling ISRO espionage case. *The Outlook* also pointed out that the ISRO case has become the burning example of the unprofessional manner in which Indian intelligence agencies function. Quoting CBI, it maintained how an innocuous-looking case of a foreign national extending a visa was blown out of proportion into typical espionage case.

While a section of Malayalam media personnel had come out of the stereotype stories on ISRO case, the large majority of them, influenced by the approach of the powerful managements or their corporate interests continued to play up the espionage story by inventing new stories packed with titillating anecdotes. The intellectuals, human/civil rights activists and literary figures remain divided: those ultra-left activists who considered Karunakaran as their bête noire since long targeted him and Srivastava, a set of human rights activists by highlighting the plight of incarcerated Maldivian women and others demanded justice to the victims and noted Malayalam writers like Paul Zacharia described the episode as black spot for the press and people of Kerala.

The visual media, by and large, toed the line of the vernacular print media and telecast live fancied stories on the main accused, whenever they appeared in public. But there were exceptions too. At national level, Sony channel in 1998 telecast a serial with characters almost on the lines of the key accused in ISRO spy case. In Kerala, the Asianet played a pivotal role to bring out the distortions and contradictions in the case and the plight of the accused, especially the two Maldivian ladies. The channel, through live interviews of the close relations of the arrested accused and special programmes, tried to give a more realistic picture of the ISRO case, demolishing many myths and mysteries connected with the case.

Ironically, those media personnel who questioned the commonly shared belief within the herd and showed the guts to say that the emperor has no clothes have to bear the brunt of all those who built up an espionage case out of nothing. They had to deal with a few libel cases filed by certain police officers aggrieved by the story or the so-called intellectuals or activists inspired by patriotism. Shekhar Gupta, the editor and publisher of *India Today*, Tripthi (editor, *Savvy* magazine), Rajasekharan Nair (author, *Spies from Space*), Jacob George (reporter, *India Today*), etc., were a few such media personnel who were dragged into such litigations. Ram Jethmalani, a renowned legal luminary of the SC, who charges lakhs for each appearance, was engaged by the some of the petitioners in a couple of such cases.

Moreover, those media personnel who remained untouchable to the mainstream media had to face general opprobrium among sections of the intelligentsia and journalists who played in the hands of the perpetrators of the spy story in building up malicious propaganda campaign against them. Many of these media men or intelligentsia were branded as those in the payroll of the then PM Narasimha Rao or agents working for foreign intelligence agencies betraying the interests of the nation. There was orchestrated propaganda and campaign against Asianet linking up the alleged connections of their higher-ups with the Soviet Union/Russia.

The ISRO espionage story is a typical example of how the media can be effectively used or say misused to build up public opinion or in the construction of consensus on controversial issues. In this case, three distinct set of media personnel, namely those purely guided by the circulation and commercial interests of their publications, those controlled and guided by political mentors and finally those overconcerned by the slogans of national security and patriotism, worked in tandem. Instead of strenuously struggling to gather inputs for the stories, they had an added advantage to get the required information or inputs from the police or the other investigation agencies. If the words of the special investigation officer, as revealed in his book *Fearless* can be believed, even the senior echelons of the police played dubious role in leaking out such information to their close vernacular media contacts.

The scenario was not different in the case of intelligence and other agencies associated with the case. Once Karunakaran became the target, his rivals within the party having a network of contacts in these agencies could easily tap their services. A group of media men loyal to these leaders acted as pivot in the disinformation campaign which like a tornado swept away Karunakaran from seats of power. Added to this was the role of self-ordained brigades of patriotism and nationalism who too could easily find their cronies in these agencies to get desired information to feed their band of journalists.

Thus, the media instead of functioning as a true watchdog of the society played second fiddle to the vicious agenda of the key players of the game. Moreover, the media's preferences to go along with those of the establishment and those wielding power had also influenced its style of reporting and filing special stories related to the case. Never did the media pause for a moment to ask questions about the veracity of the inputs that they received. Instead, they treated everything as gospel truth which they presented to reader as juicy stories fuelled by their own imagination and fantasies. That was their greatest mistake.

An equally serious mistake was the subservience of the sections of the media to play in the hands of those who always tried to justify their omissions and commissions in the ISRO case. They were instrumental in planting false stories to malign the image of all those opposed to the conventional wisdom of the espionage. Even the journalistic fraternity was not spared in such operations. A few among them played the role of public interest litigants or *benami* litigants defending the delinquent police officers or demanding the reinvestigation of the ISRO spy case. Even a couple of them ventured into publishing books in Malayalam by merely cataloguing shared IRs of the accused, official communications at police hierarchy level and other documents with the sole objective to defend the police officers or agencies responsible for framing up ISRO espionage case.

The media to a great extent has been used by such officers/agencies to proclaim their revelations that had come in the form of autobiographies or literature on the issue. Several books have been written on ISRO espionage, probably to glorify or justify the role played by different key players or their lobbies in this murkier drama. The first book *Open Secrets*[37] was penned by Late M. K. Dhār, Joint DIB; his book mainly targeted CBI allegedly for sabotaging the espionage case. There were many takers of this theory which was even promoted by sections of investigators who tried to wash off their hands from their omissions and commissions.

. . . .

[37] Maloy Krishna Dhar, *Open Secrets: India's Intelligence Unveiled* (New Delhi: Manas Publications, 2005).

Perhaps, this was succinctly put by V. S. Achuthanandan, the former CM of Kerala, while releasing the book *Nirbhayam* (Fearless),[38] another book on ISRO spy case authored by the investigator Siby Mathews, IPS, as 'it still remained a mystery whether the ISRO spy case which rocked Kerala in the mid-90s was a truth or myth'.[39] He rightly added that the author left the question unanswered in the book. The book was published during the time Nambi Narayanan had filed libel suits against the investigation officer for falsely implicating and arresting him in ISRO espionage case.

In the book, he states that there was pressure from the IB to arrest IGP Srivastava which he, as the investigation officer, had prevented. 'The reason for the IB's move is still unclear', he says in the book. But in the same vein, he highlighted that K. Karunakaran with whom Srivastava had close connections was the worst victim of the case, as he had to relinquish the CM's post as fallout of the case. The book also mentions suspicions of a conspiracy against Karunakaran led by former Congress CM Oommen Chandy in connivance with the top bishops in the state.

At the same time, he is silent on whether the arrest of Nambi Narayanan was at the instance of IB or not. In this regard, CBI had rightly observed that 'it was unprofessional on his part to have ordered indiscriminate arrests of top ISRO scientists who played a key role in successful launching of satellites in the space and thereby caused unavoidable mental and physical agony to them'.[40] And above all, a seasoned professional investigator with a record of cracking almost one dozen sensational cases in Kerala should not have been easily carried away with the whims and fancies of a central agency.

....

[38] Dr Siby Mathews, *Nirbhayam* (Malayalam) (Trivandrum: Green Books, 2017).
[39] *The Hindu*, 'ISRO Spy Case a Mystery: VS' (2018, 10 June). Trivandrum.
[40] Civil Appeal Nos. 6637–6638 of 2018, SC dated 14 September 2018 (quoted in the judgement).

The autobiography of Nambi Narayanan *Ormakalude brahmanapadam*[41] (Malayalam) and *The Orbit of Memories* (English) succinctly counters many of these claims. This book reveals the dreadful episode on how a spy is virtually created at the instance of a set of Kerala Police officials and IB sleuths with political nexus. Reproducing CBI report that had declared the ISRO spy case as false and quoting the decisions of the high court and the SC including the acquittal of all the six accused, the book raises certain crucial questions: Who created the false case? For what purpose and who all are behind it? The beleaguered scientist demands a thorough probe to bring out the truth behind the involvement of an external influence in fabricating a case, especially in the light of the undue delay of 13 years in developing an indigenous cryogenic engine by our country.

The alleged involvement of an external agency is the main focus of J. Rajasekharan Nair's book *Spies from Space*.[42] The main surmise of this book is that the tentacles of American intelligence agencies that have spread world over with sinister strategy to strangulate Indian space technology were behind this spy story, in which the IB sleuths knowingly or unknowingly had fallen in their trap. The espionage story, according to the author, had antagonized the RSA, which otherwise would have helped India acquire the cryogenic technology even after America had sabotaged the agreement between India and Russia for the transfer of technology.

> This technically absurd terminology was used by IB with a purpose: to divert the attention from the commercial angle. In the process, IB labelled ISRO as a defence research centre. The label America and Pakistan have been trying hard all these years to paste on ISRO now stand engraved in it.

. . . .

[41] Nambi Narayanan, *Ormakalude Bhramanapadham* (Malayalam) (Kottayam: DC Books, 2018).
[42] J. Rajsekharan Nair, *Spies from Space* (New Delhi: Konark Publishers, 1998).

Obviously, the ISRO espionage case had been written and moulded in many ways in media in line with the imagination, intentions and interests of the contributors or authors, which in many respects are unable to unfold the myth and mysteries surrounding the case. In that process, different theories—international conspiracy linking CIA or KGB, political conspiracy and professional jealousies and turf battles—have been floated making the story murkier. The actual truth lies in the midst of such cacophony consciously created by such players, but there will always be a light at the end of the tunnel in which the truth would sparkle like a shining star in the clouded sky!

BATTLE OF ARMAGEDDON AND THE FINAL JUDGEMENT

16

It was like the battle of Armageddon, a historic legal battle by Nambi Narayanan for over two decades against the alleged perpetrators of his arrest and humiliation. The lord who ultimately revealed his power in the interest of the distressed man was none but the SC of India. It was on 14 September 2018 when the almighty lord in trinity in flowing black gowns descended and occupied their seats. The air was filled with great suspense and anxiety. The victims and their alleged tormentors eagerly waited for the final judgement.

Just a couple of days back, in the garden city of Bangalore, K. Chandrasekharan, the bearded man with sparkling eyes, one of the victims of the case was struggling with life and death, in his Hebbal Hospital room. Whenever the TV screen in his room flashed any breaking news, his weak fainted eyes searched for the news that he had been waiting to hear for two decades. But the cruel fate was unkind to him; he slipped into a coma just hours before the lords delivered the final judgement.

But in the same city of Bangalore, S. K. Sharma, the labour contractor from Bangalore and a close friend of Chandrasekharan, another accused of the case acquitted in 1998 and fighting against cancer, was fortunate to know the final judgement. On the aftermath of the SC judgement, Sharma who had been continuing his long fight since 1998 for compensation and clear his name in public was hopeful to get justice. But his hopes were never fulfilled when he passed away on 1 November 2018, leaving his wife and two grown-up daughters.

Down in the South, in the capital city of God's own country, Nambi Narayanan, the crusader of the battle with his wife and other family members was eagerly waiting for the final judgement. He was optimistic that the lords would do justice to him. On the contrary, in the same city, the alleged tormentors were passing through anxious moments to know whether the lords would direct to initiate any criminal proceedings against them.

The three-member bench of the SC headed by Chief Justice Dipak Misra delivered the judgement on an appeal filed by Nambi Narayanan against the order passed by the division bench of the Kerala High Court. The division bench overturned the decision of the single judge who had overruled the order of the state government declining to take appropriate action against the police officers on the grounds of delay and lapses.

The judgement was historic in many respects. It was for the first time that the apex court upheld the concept of constitutional liability of the state to pay compensation to the victims in lieu of the acts of omissions and commissions from the part of the state super structures. Thus, the state of Kerala under whose jurisdiction the erred police officers functioned was directed to pay a sum of ₹50 lakh towards compensation to the appellant. The Court further cleared that the appellant can proceed with the pending civil suit wherein he has asked for more compensation and further ordered the constitution of a committee for obtaining factual scenario and to find out ways and means to take appropriate steps against erring officials. The committee to be headed by Justice D. K. Jain, a former Judge of SC, will consist one officer each nominated by the central and the state governments.

While deciding the case, the SC has arrived at the conclusions based on the findings of the final report of the CBI and a number of landmark judgements⁴³ on arrest, custodial torture, mental agony and right to life with dignity and so on. It has given a broader interpretation to the concept of torture as succinctly laid down by Adriana P. Bartow as:

> Torture is a wound in the soul so painful that sometimes you can almost touch it, but is also so intangible that there is no way to heal it. Torture is anguish squeezing your chest, cold as ice and heavy as a stone paralyzing as sleep and as dark as abyss. Torture is despair, fear and rage and hate. It is a desire to kill and destroy including yourself.⁴⁴

The investigators, according to the Court, had violated the concept of due process of law.

> The criminal law was set in motion without any basis. It was initiated, if anyone was allowed to say, of some kind of fancy or notion. The liberty and dignity of appellant which are basic to human rights were jeopardized as he was taken into custody despite all glory of the past; he was compelled to face cynical abhorrence. This situation invites public law remedy for grant of compensation for the violation of fundamental rights enshrined under Article 21 of the constitution.⁴⁵

Thus, the Court reached the final conclusion as:

> There can be no scintilla of doubt that the appellant a successful scientist with national reputation has been compelled to undergo immense humiliation. The lackadaisical attitude of the police to arrest anyone and put him in police custody has made the appellant to suffer ignominy. The dignity of a person is shocked

. . . .

[43] Japani Sahoo vs Chandra Sekhar Mohanty; D. K. Vasu vs State of West Bengal.
[44] Justice A. S. Anand, VIIIth International Symposium on Torture (Speech; 7 SCC [Jour] 10; 1999; https://www.ebc-india.com/lawyer/articles/9907a2.htm [accessed on 30 April 2019]).
[45] Civil Appeal Nos. 6637–6638 of 2018, SC dated 14 September 2018 (https://www.sci.gov.in/supremecourt/2015/19295/19295_2015_Judgement_14-Sep-2018.pdf; accessed on 6 May 2019).

when psychopathological treatment is meted out to him. A human being cries for justice when he feels that the insensible act has crucified his self-respect. That warrants grant of compensation under public law remedy. We are absolutely conscious that a civil suit has been filed for grant of compensation. That will not debar the constitutional court to grant compensation taking recourse to public law. The Court cannot lose sight of the wrongful confinement, malicious prosecution, the humiliation and the defamation faced by the appellant.[46]

The SC judgement has demonstrated that almost quarter of a century old ISRO spy case is yet to be over. Not the erring officers alone but those who played from behind the curtain are really worried over the final round of the battle in which the key player is the Jain Committee.[47] The crucial question is whether the Committee would limit its role 'to find out the ways and means to take appropriate steps against the erring officials' or use its mandate to go into the conspiracy theories floated from various corners in connection with the case.

Apart from the international conspiracy theory which is yet to be gained credibility, the political conspiracy theory has once again gained momentum after the SC verdict. The protractors of the aforementioned theory maintain that ISRO spy case which appeared like a bolt from the blue in Kerala politics during 1994 was astutely exploited by A. K. Antony faction of Congress, using

. . . .

[46] Ibid.

[47] The SC in its judgement dated 14 September 2018 ordered the formation of Justice (Retired) D. K. Jain Committee to suggest appropriate steps required to fix accountability on erring officials who foisted espionage charges against S. Nambi Narayanan and other scientists in the ISRO spy case. Accordingly, the MHA in November 2018 has appointed two former IAS officers, namely B. K. Prasad and V. S. Senthil, to assist Justice (Retired) D. K. Jain Committee. Mr Prasad, a former additional secretary in the MHA, would be the central government nominee, whereas Sethil, who had retired as additional chief secretary of Kerala would represent the Kerala government. The MHA has not stipulated any time frame for the panel to submit its recommendations.

salacious media and other fora, to dethrone K. Karunakaran from CM's post.

In the words of Ms Padmaja Venugopal, former Kerala CM K. Karunakaran's daughter and general secretary of KPCC:

> There was a political conspiracy behind the ISRO spy case, designed to destroy her father's political career. Karunakaran was targeted by rival politicians at an opportune time, given that he was in an emotionally fragile state following the recent death of his wife Kalyanikutty Amma in 1993. There were 5 politicians, all still active in political life today, who were responsible for trapping Karunakaran in this case and orchestrating his political downfall.[48]

On the other hand, her brother K. Muraleedharan, who was recently elevated as one of the working presidents of KPCC said: 'Let the truth come out. My father did not get justice. Former PM Narasimha Rao cheated my father. He took undue haste in seeking his resignation.'[49] However, his detractors in the party interpret his stand as a tactical move to exonerate his present mentors and the real players of the game obviously to safeguard his political interests.

Cherian Philip, a prominent youth Congress leader of the 1990s and a key strategist of the faction then led by A. K. Antony, is on record that he was one among the conspirators led by Oommen Chandy (former Kerala CM and present AICC general secretary) who dragged the name of IGP Raman Srivastava, the blue-eyed boy of K. Karunakaran, into the spy case, obviously to target Karunakaran.[50]

. . . .

[48] Sharanya Gopinathan, 'Politics: There Was a Political Conspiracy to Bring Down My Father in the ISRO Case: Padmaja Venugopal', *The News Minute* (2018, 14 September).
[49] Ramesh Babu, 'Heat Yet to Settle, ISRO Case Returns to Haunt Congress in Kerala', *Hindustan Times* (2018, 14 September). Thiruvananthapuram.
[50] Cherian Philip, 'I was a Party in the Conspiracy to Topple Karunakaran Using ISRO Spy Case', *Mathrubhoomi* (2018, 14 September).

Taking a cue out of the escalating group war within Congress on ISRO spy case, the political rivals of Congress notably the CPI(M) and the Bharatiya Janata Party (BJP) strive to make maximum political mileage out of the issue. Alleging that the ISRO case was fabricated by Congress leaders and that the present leadership in Kerala is solely responsible for this, senior CPI(M) leaders of Kerala openly stated that the Congress should pay the compensation of ₹50 lakh awarded to Nambi Narayanan. The CPI(M) leadership, which successfully used the ISRO case as a powerful propaganda weapon during the 1996 assembly polls, has recently taken initiative to organize an impressive function in the state capital while presenting compensation amount to Nambi Narayanan. The CM who was present in the function paid glowing tributes to him for his great determination in this historic legal battle for justice. The government organized the function only to embarrass the present state Congress leaders who allegedly whipped up the case to oust K. Karunakaran.

Though Nambi Narayanan was happy with the verdict, the octogenarian scientist who underwent the ignominy of being branded as a spy continues his crusade to get punished the police officers allegedly who fabricated the case against him. 'Pinning the blame squarely on Siby Mathews, the then DIG of Police who led the special investigation team (SIT), he held that no police officer should go free in such cases. He is optimistic that the Judicial Committee would do justice in this regard.'[51]

On the other hand, the BJP strategy appears to use the ISRO scandal during 2019 LS poll campaign linking it with internal security and clandestine designs of international agencies to destabilize the nation under the canopy of Congress and other opposition parties. Commenting on the SC judgement, Kerala

....

[51] https://timesofindia.indiatimes.com/city/thiruvananthapuram/wanted-3-cops-who-fabricated-the-case-punished-says-nambi/articleshow/65817083.cm (accessed on 26 January 2019).

chief of the party maintained[52] that 'the espionage case was part of an international conspiracy involving international agencies including the United States of India against India developing the coveted cryogenic engine technology'. Thus, his demand is that the Judicial Commission should probe into this angle too including the role of central agencies. D. Sasikumaran, a colleague of Nambi Narayanan in ISRO and another accused in the case, held that he would depose before the Judicial Committee and submit his doubts on conspiracy theory to the Committee. However, he was critical of the approach of the hierarchy of ISRO, which instead of rectifying the doubts of police kept conscious silence throughout the ISRO spy scandal.

Both the Maldivian ladies, Mariam Rasheeda and Fauzia Hassan, who had to undergo incarceration of around three years in the ISRO spy case and now in Maldives, are happy over the SC verdict. They have plans to go to SC of India and international forums of human rights, etc., seeking compensation for illegal detention and alleged torture.

Meanwhile, the indicted police officers are under a shadow of despair and frustration. Siby Mathews, the former DGP and chief information officer, who headed the SIT kept away from the media without offering any comments to the SC verdict. S. Vijayan, who recorded the initial arrest of Maldivian ladies and now indicted by the court, alleged that he was a victim of conspiracy, whereas the third officer in the case, K. K. Joshua, who was in the SIT, felt that the apex court has made harsh remarks against him on trivial matters. The crucial question is as how the Jain Committee would finally settle the case of these officers and also the grey areas of ISRO spy story.

....

[52] https://www.thehindu.com/todays-paper/tp-national/probe-ib-role-in-isro-case-bjp/article5277231.ece?fbclid=IwAR1KwFbeUe-CU0pZlaK11P-WwU_33mDh WIOQShYUTaM_NHftag (accessed on 12 January 2019).

IN HINDSIGHT AD NAUSEAM

17

Almost after a quarter century, the ISRO espionage case continues to create strong ripples that occasionally shake the pillars of democracy such as the fourth estate, Criminal Justice System and, of course, the polity by posing serious questions on their credibility, professionalism and transparency.

There are also worthy persons who visualize the ISRO espionage with dispassionate eyes and throw much light on the realities connected with the case. Dr P. M. Nair, ex-CBI officer[53] who headed CBI investigation of the case, has recently ruled out the involvement of the Central Intelligence Agency (CIA) of the USA or the India's IB in the case. He asserted that neither former PM Narasimha Rao nor his son was linked to the case, as vigorously propagated by certain political parties and sections of media. Mr Nair has revealed a truth that ISRO scientist Nambi Narayanan and the other accused would have been in jail for at least 14 years if the case had not been entrusted to the CBI, indirectly indicating the overenthusiasm of police and other agencies in implicating them in an espionage case!

Similarly, more and more media personnel have abandoned their stereotype stories on ISRO spy case. They no longer close their eyes on the hard realities of the case. The best example is Shri T. J. S. George, an eminent journalist of international reputation, who

---

[53] *Manorama Online*, 'ISRO Espionage Case: Ex-CBI Officer Rules Out CIA, IB Link' (1998, 27 December). Available at https://english.manoramaonline.com/news/kerala/2017/12/27/spy-agencies-werent-linked-isro-case.html (accessed on 24 January 2019).

initially had genuine doubts as whether ISRO case was a myth or not. Now he is fully convinced that it was nothing but a myth, whose roots he succinctly traces as

> It all started with a Kerala Police inspector eyeing a six-foot Maldivian woman. Spurned by her, he set out to get her tied up in legal knots, then found an opportunity to file spying charges against her. The case quickly became a cause célèbre used by multiple agencies for multiple purposes.[54]

Perhaps, the aforementioned comments lucidly explain a number of crucial questions connected with ISRO espionage case: How the case started? Who were the persons behind it? What were their motives? Who were benefitted? Neither the agencies associated with the case nor the investigators nor their autobiographies could throw much light on these sensitive questions.

In fact, through the pages of this book, a serious attempt has been made to give convincing answers to such questions by exploring the truth behind ISRO espionage case. The case started with the arrest of Mariam Rasheeda, a Maldivian lady who had overstayed in India without valid visa. The question naturally arises how this lady alone had become the target of police, especially when there were ample number of Maldivians overstaying in Trivandrum under one pretext or other. The key players of the case came out with their own reasons, but the most convincing one, as rightly highlighted by the veteran journalist, was the lewd and lascivious style of approach of the concerned police officer. Rasheeda's background as a former private of Maldivian intelligence agency, the NSS coupled with a few entries in her personal diary about the suspected activities of resident Maldivians in India, opposed to Maldivian President Abdul Gayoom, gave enough ground for the police inspector to build up his own story.

....

[54] T. J. S. George, 'Why ISRO "Spy Case" is Important?', *The New Indian Express* (2018, 7 July).

Ironically, the senior hierarchy of the police instead of correcting such aberrations by their subordinates gave green signal to them to go ahead with the case. A few senior sleuths in New Delhi and Trivandrum were ecstatic over the detection of an espionage case! After all, it was after many decades that they got a golden opportunity to burst a major espionage network in southern India, having national and international linkages!

Initially, a senior officer from Mumbai who was deputed to question the arrested Maldivian ladies could not unearth anything connected with their espionage activities. Those bosses committed to espionage theory outrightly vetoed his findings and decided to go ahead with counter-espionage operation on war footing: the so-called CI experts were summoned from different places, teams of interrogators landed at the state capital and the techies with their bugging and recording devices arrived en masse to join the operation. When the news of a major spy ring around India's space programme appeared in headlines, the personnel of other intelligence and security agencies jumped the gun. They had hijacked the entire operation for a couple of weeks virtually sidelining the police which alone has the legal powers to deal with the arrested persons.

Unfortunately, things did not change even after an SIT of Kerala Police, headed by an officer of the rank of DIG, had taken over the investigation of the case. The team, instead of independently investigating the leads and arriving at conclusions, blindly followed the disclosures or statements made by some of the accused during interrogation and failed to follow the due process of law even in the case of the arrest of senior space scientists. Such hasty decisions compelled the investigators to pad up evidence to justify their actions, which had virtually derailed the entire investigation. Thus, one of the crucial findings of CBI was that ISRO espionage case made out by the police was without foundation and was cooked up with fabricated evidence.

One pertinent question arises as to what extent the police or intelligence organizations are responsible for such professional mishaps or misdemeanours. In fact, these organizations are constituted with basic charter or purpose to safeguard the interest of the nation and the people. Basically, these are vertical organizations in which decisions taken at the hierarchy level are being enforced or implemented by the subordinate personnel at horizontal level. However, influenced by the personal agenda or interests of those at hierarchy, they deviate from their charter of duties or tasks. Unfortunately all the blame comes against the organization for all such professional lapses or aberrations.

When we explore the inside story of the ISRO espionage case, many such factors come to the fore. One major story that went around the corridors of the North Block was that ISRO spy case was the creation of a senior intelligence officer who had his personal agenda to get clear his pending application for the correction of date of birth in service records enabling him to get a couple of years more service. Alas, when the operation had boomeranged, his superannuation papers were unceremoniously delivered at his doorsteps! Another story was that a particular branch at the headquarters was keener to burst as much modules of ISI as possible so that those heading the branch would be assured of prestigious assignments within the organization and outside! Down the lane in the state Bureau, senior officers were weaving sweet dreams on their elevation to cosy posts and largesse from the headquarters in respect of special funds and logistics. Moreover, they tried to use the espionage case to cement their relations with sections of political leaders in the state.

Situation was not different in the case of state police or the SIT. On one hand, the North–South divide among the IPS officers of the state coupled with the rat race among a section of the officers to build up their career had also influenced the investigation process. The controversial IGP from the North was one of the youngest IPS officers of Kerala cadre elevated to that post. His proximity to the then CM and senior Congress leader K. Karunakaran had created more foes for him within the force and outside. Virtually, the IGP became the rallying point of attack of all detractors of Karunakaran including state ministers and MPs.

Perhaps the best example was the comments of a state minister of the UDF on the SC judgement of 1998 exonerating all the accused: 'it was imperative that Srivastava be shown the door. The people of the state were not convinced of the Police officer's innocence. Action to be taken against the super cop'.[55]

Half-baked uncorroborated information collected during interrogation or investigation was leaked out to political mentors and the media. While deposing before the CBI, even the head of the SIT cast aspersions against the then DGP for his close connections with the key functionaries of a vernacular daily from southern Kerala, which was in the forefront of publishing ISRO spy stories. On the other hand, the SIT head had also come under attack. A senior ADGP embarrassed the SIT chief, when he submitted a lengthy letter to the then DGP in April 1995 alleging that the police investigators extracted confessions to falsely implicate the IGP in the case. In fact, such internal politics and polemics in Kerala Police was one of the major factors for linking the IGP with espionage network.

Again, the personal agenda played havoc with the free and fair investigation of the case and related developments. Perhaps all agencies and bodies associated with the case, one way or other, contributed to this discernible trend. For example, intelligence agencies in their overenthusiasm to unearth a sensational espionage case in South India deviated from the established strategy and mechanisms in detecting espionage cases. Instead of discreetly pursuing any input of espionage nature by using various tradecraft tools such as surveillance, interception/monitoring/bugging, clandestine photography and profiling of suspects and their associates, the suspects of the case were detained in haste and interrogated with much fanfare.

....

[55] *The New Indian Express*, 'Political Double Speak as SC Closes Spy Case' (1998, 1 May). Trivandrum.

The fundamentals of interrogation techniques were flouted. Interrogation teams with every Tom, Dick and Harry who were bereft of professional skills or basic knowledge on space technology were hurriedly constituted to question senior space scientists of international reputation! Without proper planning or briefing, such interrogators—many new to this tradecraft mechanism—acted on their own, bullied and humiliated the accused. Not only they failed to extract any factual inputs from the accused but also they cut a sorry figure before them demonstrating their ignorance and poor knowledge. Moreover, the sanctity of this vital tradecraft tool was visibly vitiated while there were conscious efforts to make fake confessions or to put words or inputs into the mouth of the accused to weave confessional stories on desired lines!

Another serious flaw was the failure of the concerned agencies to ensure the spot verification of the disclosures made by the accused. While blindly forwarding the revelations to their higher formations, they tried to absolve themselves by offering shrewd comments that 'these disclosures were a mixture of truth, half-truth or untruth'. If they had made verification of some of the crucial disclosures at that level, the arrest of senior space scientists and other innocent persons could have been avoided. The approach of senior intelligence bosses had also come under severe criticism. Instead of making a thorough analysis of these disclosures or verifying them through other sources/channels, they drew sweeping conclusions about certain people which were officially communicated to the highest functionaries of the Government of India. Even the needle of suspicion in such official notes was ironically pointed towards the then PM of India or his close relations! Unable to retract from such conclusions or findings, they resorted to cover-up operations by using sections of media and other sources.

With the easy accessibility of secret information including the disclosures of the accused, key players of vernacular media had virtually celebrated the espionage case by serializing sensational stories with all ingredients—sex, money and foreign agents. They too had different agenda or motives: increase the circulation of publications, mould up public opinion to bolster the hidden agenda of their political mentors and highlight the impending threats to national security. Never did the media pause for a moment to ask questions about the veracity of the inputs that they received. 'It was a mad race for the juiciest story and the race went on till the sky opened.'

All hell broke loose when the political parties entered the scene with their sinister motive to exploit the ISRO spy case in line with their agenda. While a section of Congress leaders used the case to get rid of the then Congress CM K. Karunakaran, the Left parties, notably the CPI(M) used it as a political weapon to weaken the mass base of the Congress-led UDF in the state. Through orchestrated campaign propped up by sections of the print and electronic media, they had created so much hype in the case that everyone associated with it were deemed as potential spies or anti-national elements. The erratic public hurled abuses at the accused wherever they appeared; there were instances of ISRO vehicles being pelted with stones and auto-rickshaws and taxis refusing to ply for ISRO personnel.

Such public rhetoric coupled with the overriding interests of political parties—both ruling and opposition—led the Kerala Police to play a dastardly role in the case. A section of senior police officers including the SIT meekly surrendered to the whims and fancies of their political mentors and made compromises on the basics of investigation. The SIT arrested a senior scientist like Nambi Narayanan without any evidence, or any search or seizure at his residence or office. Thus, the CBI itself rejected all its findings and case diaries which 'reflect adversely on the methods and intentions of the IOs of the Kerala Police'. Moreover, the police hierarchy went ahead with the reinvestigation or further investigation of the case already investigated by the CBI and finally settled by the SC. The senior police officers who were instrumental for undertaking such actions apparently flouting the due process of law were liberally rewarded by their political masters. The officer who initiated the reinvestigation of the case in 1996 at the instance of the CPI(M)-led LDF had later became the DGP, whereas the SIT head, despite having a couple of pending cases against him, was appointed as the chief information officer of Kerala!

The public or media trial of the accused, according to some legal circles, had impacted the decisions of the august institutions such as judiciary. Thus, judicial decision, purely based on uncorroborated electronic evidence, was made on crucial issues such as the genuineness of video cassettes containing the confessional statements of some of the accused during interrogation. Had the concerned court stuck to the established judicial or legal norms in evaluating such pieces of evidence and taken a more judicious approach in such matters, an entirely different picture would have emerged in the police investigation including the question of arrest of scientists and others. The SC has rightly highlighted these aspects while deciding a petition filed by the CBI seeking to expunge certain references made by the lower court in this connection.

In fact, the hype created in the case had thoroughly demoralized the scientific community which helplessly watched the plight of senior space scientists implicated in espionage case. Many of them feared that they too can become easy targets of security and law enforcement agencies. Thus, it was almost after two years since the occurrence of the case that senior scientists like Satish Dhawan and U. R. Rao (both former chairman, ISRO), Yash Pal (former chairman, UGC), R. Narasimhan (former director, National Aerospace Laboratories), A. S. Chandrasekhar (former scientist, ISRO) and T. N. Seshan (former additional secretary, Space Department, Chief Election Commissioner) openly came out urging the government to end the harassment of Nambi Narayanan and family in name of reported ISRO espionage case. Seshan made it clear that Nambi had made exemplary service to ISRO, especially in developing cryogenic engine technology. In this regard, the words of Nambi Narayanan appear to be much relevant.

> The scientific community in this country is highly intelligent and hardworking but lack even the basic knowledge of simple matters

like law, Fundamental rights and so on. In other words, we are so much occupied with our time bound work that we don't find time to understand these trivial matters and as a result we get taken for a ride, sometimes. It is very important to realize the words like patriotism, national security, terrorism and so on can be loosely used by some of the law enforcing agencies simply to arrest a person.[56]

No doubt, broadening the horizons of the knowledge on matters such as national security, law enforcement and fundamental rights and so on to a great extent can help scientists and others falling victims to professional lapses of law enforcement or other agencies. At the same time, such measures would also help to accelerate the systemic changes within their establishments, particularly in the areas of internal security, operating procedures, etc., that would thwart any attempts of espionage or security hazards. In both the cases, the ultimate beneficiary no doubt would be the particular scientific organization. It is now everyone's guess how the espionage story retarded our advancements in space technology. Had there not been the infamous ISRO case, we would have developed cryogenic technology almost a decade ago. Perhaps, the words of Kumar Chellappan rightly point towards this truth.

> The ISRO spy case of 1994 not only finished the careers of India's two exceptionally brilliant space scientists by implicating them as spies but also put the country's cryogenic engine development programme on hold for more than 19 years. The programme could have saved India millions of dollar.[57]

That brings us to a crucial question how cataclysms like the ISRO spy case that spoil the lives of innocent persons and hamper the progress and development of the nation can be averted.

....

[56] Nambi Narayanan, 'Will the NHRC Take Notice?', *Express Magazine* (Spotlight; 1998, 27 September).
[57] Kumar Chellappan, 'True Lies', *Sunday Pioneer* (2013, 8 December).

In fact, there are thousands of unfortunate souls languishing in various jails for no faults of their own, but due to the omissions and commissions of the key players of our Criminal Justice System. The need of the hour is to enforce adequate mechanisms that would effectively check the tendency of the law enforcing agencies to fabricate false cases against individuals, especially on the grounds of organized crimes such as terrorism, extremism, espionage and so on. There is a growing tendency to extensively use draconian legislations against the victims, which incapacitate them to seek timely judicial intervention to prove their innocence. By the time some kind of justice prevails, the victims remain incarcerated as under trials for years; their families which are socially ostracized, condemned and humiliated are virtually ruined for no mistake of their own.

Such unfortunate things happen unabated because of the over-confidence of the state representatives that the arms of justice would never reach them by virtue of the protection that they enjoy in the existing system. Very often, they use the protective shield of the concept of doctrine of sovereignty or the legal jargon of good faith defined in Section 52 of the Indian Penal Code (IPC). To demolish such unfounded thinking among law enforcement personnel, there is urgent need to demonstrate that the law enforcing agencies cannot escape from the clutches of law if they have misused their power and authority.

It is equally important that accountability and professionalism should be ensured in the case of our secret agencies which are not constituted under any statute of the legislature. Moreover, as their charter of duties is totally clandestine and secret, there should be effective monitoring mechanisms to ensure that their operations and activities are genuine, truthful and unbiased. Perhaps, these unique and essential features of any intelligence set-up are succinctly incorporated by the CIA of the USA in their definition of intelligence as timely truth well told.

A number of committees such as Henderson Brooks Committee (1962) B. S. Raghavan Committee (1965 and 1966), L. P. Singh

Committee (1975–1977), K. Sankaran Nair Committee (1980–1982), Kargil Review Committee and G. C. Saxena Special Task Force (1999–2000), Ram Pradhan Committee (2008) and Pradhan–Haldar–Narasimham Committee (2009), etc., had gone deep into such matters as how real-time intelligence that could avert major intelligence failures could be generated. These committees have gone into the functioning of our intelligence agencies including their failures and successes. They came out with a number of recommendations to strengthen these organizations to meet the new challenges in the internal security front. Over the years, some changes had been made in respect of the recruitment, training and deployment of personnel along with some efforts to make these bodies tech-savvy with the formation of new outfits such as National Technical Research Organisation (NTRO).

Ironically, these committees had conveniently ignored the core aspect of the accountability of the intelligence agencies obviously due to the powerful lobbying by intelligence mandarins. The political leadership too had succumbed to such pressures and adopted a strategy of dilly-dallying on such matters. In 1989, the move initiated by senior BJP MP Jaswant Singh,[58] as the chairman of the Parliamentary Estimates Committee to bring the RAW, IB and CBI under the ambit of parliamentary scrutiny was scuttled by the same lobby.[59]

Similarly, a private bill (The Intelligence Services [Powers and Regulation] Bill 2011)[60] piloted by Manish Tiwari, Congress spokesperson and MP, in Lok Sabha to regulate the functioning and use of power by the Indian intelligence agencies within and outside India and to provide for the coordination, control and oversight

....

[58] Arthur G. Rubinoff, 'India's New Subject-Based Parliamentary Standing Committees', *Asian Survey* 36, no. 7 (1996, July): 723–738.
[59] B. R. Srikant, Rajesh Joshi and Venu Menon, 'ISRO Case—IB Imagined Spy-Ring'.
[60] 'The Intelligence Services (Powers and Regulation) Bill, 2011' (Bill No. 23 of 2011).

of such agencies failed to see the light of the day. In fact, the draft bill contained a number of provisions such as formulation of charter for each agency to prevent poaching on each other's turf, embargo on activities in furtherance of the interests of any political party or coalition of political parties or other such interest groups and the formation of bodies such as National Intelligence and Security Oversight Committee, Intelligence Ombudsman and National Intelligence Tribunal to ensure accountability of intelligence operations and check the professional omissions and commissions. One of the most significant provisions in the bill was that no intelligence chief could be considered for gubernatorial appointments or reappointment to any post under the state except as an advisor to the Government of India after retirement.

Such ban or a cooling period of three to five years for all superannuated officers of the rank of ADGP/DGP in police and similar ranks in other law enforcement and investigative agencies for appointments to statutory or semi-statutory bodies of the state is another mechanism to check the misuse of powers by such personnel at the verge of retirement. There is growing tendency among sections of such senior echelons of the law enforcement bodies to appease the ruling establishment or the political masters in power so as to ensure their post-retirement assignments. In that process, they compromise with the due process of law or brutally negate the rule of law so that innocent persons become the victims. Perhaps, the best example is the ISRO espionage case in which such personal or professional agenda of a set of officers virtually torpedoed many vital aspects of Criminal Justice System.

The print and electronic media particularly at vernacular level easily fall in the trap of the senior echelons of the law enforcement agencies or the political bosses who have their own axe to grind in sensational cases. Usually, they take the inputs received from such sources at face value and seldom try to ascertain their veracity. Instead, they build up and serialize sensitive investigation stories which create a mass psyche in which the general public fail to identity myth and reality or truth and untruth! Unfortunately, the hype created by the media, in many cases, influence almost all major organs of the Criminal Justice System including judiciary, as a result of which, justice is denied for the victims. The need of the hour is that the media—both the print and electronic—should develop more accountability in respect of their stories. They should not fall prey to the mechanisms of organized groups or agencies to use them as a potential weapon to perpetrate their dubious designs or vested interests.

About the Author

K. V. Thomas (aka Toms Kara) was closely associated with the different phases of the 1994 ISRO espionage case. A law graduate from University of Kerala, he has over 36 years of distinguished career in IB, MHA, Government of India, in various capacities in different parts of India including the far-flung insurgency-affected areas of the north-east. K. V. Thomas superannuated from IB in 2010 as Assistant Director.

For his outstanding contributions to the Bureau, he was awarded with President's Police Medal for distinguished service (2008) and Indian Police Medal for meritorious service (1996), besides special awards of the Bureau for his outstanding professional contributions in the field of internal security. The National Police Academy, Hyderabad, awarded him Police Fellowship in 1997 for undertaking a research project on policing which he successfully completed in 1998.

He is now fully engaged in bringing out quality publications in various subjects, especially internal security/law enforcement, human rights and insurgency. He has authored four books: *Human Rights, Terrorism and Policing in India* (1999), *Policing in 21st Century—Myth, Realities and Challenges* (2012), *Left-Wing Extremism and Human Rights* (2014) and *Kerala: Insurgency for Politics* (2018) besides publishing a large number of research-based articles in leading publications.

It's great to see a book capturing the magical journey of Indian football being written. I wish *India's Football Dream* and its authors Mr Shantanu Gupta and Mr Nikhil Sharma the very best, and hope it serves as a tool to educate every Indian about the 'beautiful game' in our country.

Praful Patel,
President, All India Football Federation

A book about how Football has grown as one of the most loved sports in India.

For special offers on this and other books from SAGE, write to marketing@sagepub.in

Explore our range at
www.sagepub.in

Paperback
978-93-532-8305-6